To my good

King Young

from

Chief C. H. Anderson

Aug 19, 1960

Beverly Hills Is My Beat

BEVERLY HILLS

IS

MY BEAT

by   Clinton H. Anderson

Chief, Beverly Hills Police Dept.

Prentice-Hall, Inc.

Englewood Cliffs, N. J.

CONTENTS

1. RICH MAN'S TOWN   1

2. CLARA BOW'S MIDNIGHT VISITOR   18

3. HOW PATROLS CATCH CROOKS   30

4. ALMOST A HERO   39

5. NO PARADISE FOR POLICEMEN   50

6. WOLVES AND WOMEN   60

7. LANA AND JOHNNY   69

8. A GALLERY OF STYLISH SWINDLERS   76

9. SOCIETY RACKETEERS   86

10. I REMEMBER WALBURGA   96

11. THE BUTLER DID IT   107

12. BURGLARS IN THE HILLS   118

13. UNWELCOME VISITORS   131

14. WHO KILLED BUGSY SIEGEL   139

15. THE MAD BOMBER OF BEVERLY HILLS   148

16. CHARLIE CHAPLIN'S GIRL FRIEND   156

17.   FATHER DIVINE'S "HEAVEN"—
      BEVERLY HILLS BRANCH   163

18.   TROUBLE IN PARADISE   169

19.   ROBBERS FOR HIRE   176

20.   GOLD PLATED DELINQUENTS   184

21.   CITY OF BROKEN DREAMS   193

22.   TELLERS OF TALES   200

23.   GOOD POLICEMEN ARE BORN   210

one

RICH MAN'S

TOWN

The UNLUCKIEST CROOK I EVER MET WAS A BURGLAR who fell asleep under a bed in Beverly Hills. He was the kind of criminal who has made police work unique in this exclusive community. Hiding in a master bedroom, with nothing to do but wait for his victims to retire for the night, he yielded to the thick luxury of the wall-to-wall carpeting. He was snoring peacefully on the floor when we arrived to arrest him.

Later he was to be one of the last men hanged in California for murder, but that is a story for another chapter. I remember the sleepy burglar because he found his brief encounter with life among the millionaires too rich for his blood. However, I've been handling millionaires and movie stars and other gold-plated types for more than 30 years as a Beverly Hills policeman, and it's been fascinating, honestly.

Not everybody here is a millionaire, of course, but we have enough of them to make this city of sunshine, palm trees and swimming pools the wealthiest community of its size in the United States, and possibly the world. Seventy-five per cent of

1

our citizens are wealthy, and some of them are downright rich, living in mansions behind locked and guarded gates.

We have more celebrities in Beverly Hills than you can shake a nightstick at. Fringing the canyons and hilltops of the city are the homes of some 200 of the biggest "names" in motion pictures and television, dozens of famous producers, directors and writers, composers, musicians, song-writers, international society leaders, oil and industrial millionaires who commute to offices in New York, and world travelers who are forever bringing home new ideas on police methods from Australia, Hong Kong, Fiji, and other remote spots.

Back in 1919 when the movie stars began building show-place homes in the foothills west of Hollywood, Douglas Fairbanks, Senior, suggested putting a wall around our little six-square-mile city to keep it exclusive. The wall never materialized, but an invisible economic wall nevertheless set Beverly Hills apart. Mary Pickford, Gloria Swanson, Charlie Chaplin, Will Rogers, Harold Lloyd, Tom Mix, Marion Davies, John Barrymore, Carl Laemmle, Louis B. Mayer and other movie "greats" were early settlers. Later came industrialists and millionaires, men with names like Doheny, Firestone, Hearst, Cord, Nash and Pauley.

Their homes and others built during the years have made Beverly Hills a tourist attraction. Sightseeing buses daily pass Harold Lloyd's estate in Benedict Canyon and Pickfair, Mary Pickford's hilltop home on 20 landscaped acres. Fred Astaire is her next-door neighbor on Summit Drive. Sidewalk vendors along Sunset Boulevard do a steady business selling guide maps to movie-star homes to the 3,000,000 tourists who come here every year by private automobile. And even if many of our famous homes are screened by high walls and trees, and the guide maps often are out-of-date, the city's other residences make the trip worth while.

White-pillared Colonials, tile-roofed Spanish homes in pinks and blues, glass-walled moderns and low-slung ranch houses border winding streets lined by palm trees 60 feet in height. Within the city's estates are artificial waterfalls, indoor fountains, private trout pools, inlaid marble floors transported from European castles, swimming pools ranging up to $100,000 in price, gold-plated bathroom fixtures and private motion-picture projection booths for home screenings.

One hillside home is surrounded by a large collection of life-size imported marble statues, some of them under individual shelters. Another mansion and its grounds cost the owner a cool $3,000,000. Many of these estates are guarded around the clock by private watchmen and elaborate alarm systems.

As the hub of an area of 25 square miles of fine homes, Beverly Hills has become one of the smartest shopping districts in America. Prices in many of the fashionable shops along Wilshire Boulevard, Rodeo Drive, Beverly Drive and neighboring streets are sky high. Juel Park has nice lace negligees at $1500 each; Mr. Rex sells cerulean mink hats for $550, and you can pick up a 24-carat emerald-cut diamond from Ruser for just $200,000. Children's toys? Uncle Bernie's Toy Menagerie has fancy stuffed tigers at $400 each.

At Christmas, corner drugstores do a department-store business in $200 gold cigarette lighters and $185-a-bottle perfumes. Style shows here frequently have furs and jewels on display valued at more than $1,000,000, and private detectives as well as police are in attendance.

Although non-resident shoppers support much of this retail luxury, the local economic picture is rather rosy. Blessed with the sixth highest per-capita income in the United States, Beverly Hills has an average per-family buying power of $10,487, more branch offices of New York Stock Exchange members than any other city our size, and approximately $400,000,000 on deposit in our banks. They still tell the story about the good-hearted women of the city who gathered Christmas baskets to give to the poor—and then couldn't find anybody in Beverly Hills to give them to!

Lawyers and doctors love us. We have almost a thousand attorneys here, although our only courts are small municipal ones. We have 650 medical men, including many expensive psychiatrists, but no hospitals or cemeteries. Few babies have ever been born in Beverly Hills, and no one that I know of is buried inside our city limits.

When local residences are for sale, the "For Sale" sign on the front lawn is restricted by law to a discreet 10-by-20 inches in size, and real estate is expensive. We have 30,000 trees registered and cared for by the Park Department, almost one for every citizen. Much of this planned beauty originated with Burton E. Green, the founder of Beverly Hills, who established a tree nursery when he launched the first subdivision here in 1907.

We like it quiet in Beverly Hills and have won national awards for our anti-noise campaign. Citations are handed out to automobile drivers who honk their horns unnecessarily and to citizens who make undue noise after 10 P.M. or before 8 A.M. We don't allow construction work to start before 8 A.M., and never on Sunday except by special permit.

People joke about the absence of pedestrians on our fine residential streets, but since the average family here has two automobiles and two telephones there is little need to walk except for exercise. Our patrolmen admittedly are inquisitive about strangers walking in certain districts, yet there are many regular pedestrians the public never see who are well known to the police. We have several writers and songwriters who get their inspiration while pacing the streets at night, and we have show-business veterans who from force of habit get up at 6 P.M. and stay up all night. The late L. B. Mayer, head of Metro-Goldwyn-Mayer studios, used to love his evening strolls here. Samuel Goldwyn, another movie pioneer, and his wife are still among our best-known walkers.

We don't discourage pedestrians we know, like the be-whiskered gentleman in a weatherbeaten Stetson and creased cowboy boots who hikes through our estates; he is an Arizona rancher living here. And we don't bother the lone woman who walks the streets every morning between two and four o'clock, rain or shine, always in the gutters, avoiding the sidewalks. Every patrolman on night duty knows her. We also have

4

a friendly word for the wealthy woman who lives in a large house surrounded by an electrically-wired fence, with the grounds illuminated all night long. We know she was badly frightened by a criminal in her youth.

Very little happens in Beverly Hills that the world doesn't hear about, particularly in the movie colony. Incidents occurring 10 miles away often become "Beverly Hills" in newspaper headlines because of the glamor attached to the name. Louella Parsons, Hedda Hopper and Sheilah Graham, all local residents, and several hundred other Hollywood correspondents representing newspapers all over the world help make Beverly Hills the fourth or fifth most active news center in the United States, exceeded only by Washington, D.C., New York City, and one or two of the largest cities. Newspaper cartoonists like the late George McManus, of "Jiggs and Maggie" fame, and Jimmy Murphy have lived and worked here.

We take our celebrities in stride. Gary Cooper entering his office at Wilshire Boulevard and Beverly Drive, Jimmy Stewart taking his twins to Sunday School, or Lucille Ball window-shopping, hardly get a second look; anywhere else they would draw crowds. Although our movie residents are internationally famous they are not as powerful in local society as other citizens whose wealth is the product of generations but whose names are seldom seen because they dislike publicity.

Through the years our Mayors and City Councilmen have been citizens of means and reputation, millionaires and retired generals among them, who serve the city without pay. Even our school-crossing guards, traffic policemen for children going to and from schools, are frequently retired wealthy men who take these jobs just to have something worthwhile to do. One of our guards recently requested a three months leave of absence. He was leaving for Europe, but he first wanted to make sure that his job would be waiting for him when he came back.

Beverly Hills has an international flavor. Distinguished visitors from London, Rome, Paris and other world capitals frequent our luxury hotels, and many foreign notables arrive incognito to transact international business. Through the years I've watched members of the British royal family, European rulers, princes of Saudi Arabia, Indian maharajahs, the Shah of Iran, the Premier of Cambodia and many others come and go.

We had a small diplomatic problem when the King of Jordan and the Israeli Ambassador were our guests simultaneously, but luckily both gentlemen enjoyed their visits without incident. Former President Aleman of Mexico and ex-King Farouk's mother and sister own homes in Beverly Hills, and a number of representatives of foreign governments live here. Hardly a week goes by that I'm not expected to make an official appearance at some function to meet visiting celebrities.

My outstanding diplomatic achievement of 1959 occurred when I waved off one of my efficient young patrolmen as he was about to give a traffic ticket to the Duke of Windsor. The Duke and Duchess were double-parked outside the Beverly Hills Hotel while loading aides, dogs and luggage into two station wagons to continue their tour of California. Since our famous visitors had got lost twice the day before while motoring through our winding streets and needed help in finding their way out of town, I felt they were entitled to this consideration. As it was, I got razzed for this small courtesy by an irate housewife who wrote me a scorching letter. She had paid a fine for an identical offense, she said, so why not the Duke of Windsor who could better afford it?

If the Duke had received a citation he would have had to pay it. Nobody can fix a traffic ticket in Beverly Hills. There are so many influential people here that the police department cannot afford to play favorites. Years ago the judges and the police worked out an escape-proof traffic ticket plan. Our policy is so well known now that everybody pays, or goes to court.

In earlier days when it was customary for cities to give prominent citizens honorary badges we sometimes had trouble with them. I remember two privileged residents whose Cadillacs collided at a busy intersection. Both men stepped out of their cars to argue the matter while traffic piled up around them. One driver flashed an honorary police captain's badge, and his opponent countered with a gold-plated deputy sheriff's emblem, also honorary. They were about to arrest each other when I arrived on the scene. I settled the argument by pointing out that I could arrest both of them for obstructing traffic and disturbing the peace. "All you have to do is to exchange names, addresses and license numbers in the usual manner and get your automobiles off the street immediately," I advised them. Both men quickly saw the wisdom of my position, and traffic soon was flowing smoothly again. We abandoned honorary badges long ago, and many other cities have done likewise.

I remember another troublesome honorary official, an oil millionaire who rated a police siren on his automobile by virtue of his appointment to a State commission by the Governor. Unfortunately, he liked to drink to excess, and in his gayer moods would have his chauffeur drive him around Beverly Hills after midnight with the siren screaming, waking up everybody in town. Abuses of this kind resulted in a State law prohibiting the use of sirens on private vehicles.

I have found that millionaires, even as you and I, have all the human frailties. They will resort to all kinds of dodges in an attempt to save a few dollars, particularly in coping with our traffic laws. One wealthy stock broker with a pair of high-power binoculars got away with overtime parking on a residential street near the business district by a plan which must have kept him rather occupied. He would park his car, then watch it from his office window through binoculars. When he saw a traffic officer mark his tire he would wait two hours and then move the car just before the officer was due to check tires again. By this stratagem he got free parking for considerable periods of time. However, a homeowner on the street complained about certain cars parking constantly in front of his house, and we set a trap for the culprit. Instead of marking tires, a traffic officer in a police car a short distance away noted the arrival time of automobiles left on the street and ticketed

7

those which were still there two hours later. One of them was the broker's car. Outraged by what he called police "deception," the broker complained to the Mayor that we had been "unethical" in not marking his tire, and revealed how he had kept watch on it with binoculars. But he had to pay the $2 fine.

On one summer afternoon as I was sitting in the office of a prominent attorney I was startled by the loud ringing of an alarm clock. His secretary promptly leaped up and left the room. When she returned she explained: "I had to move the boss's car. He's parked in a two-hour zone!"

Another artful dodger got rid of an overtime parking ticket by a fiendishly simple ruse. He merely put the ticket on the windshield of the car nearest his and drove away. He gambled that his neighbor would pay the ticket without checking the license number which the traffic officer had written on it, and he almost got away with it. The innocent victim showed up at the station to pay the ticket, but protested that he did not deserve it. In checking, we noticed the discrepancy in the license numbers and nabbed the real offender.

Handling millionaires is sometimes a headache for the police. Two prominent citizens quarreling over a barking dog can be more troublesome than a couple of longshoremen slugging each other on Pier Nine. A policeman can stop a fistfight with a nightstick, but when he gets in the middle of a millionaires' feud he has a more sophisticated problem. We have had some famous feuds in Beverly Hills, most of them rather silly. It takes remarkably little to start a neighborhood fuss, noisy children or dogs will do it, and we have had some Homeric battles over the ownership of hedges. Local surveyors have picked up small fortunes resurveying property lines.

I remember two wealthy families who got into a wrangle over some rose bushes between their estates. The trouble started when one family's gardener accidentally flooded the bushes. The neighbor's wife charged the damage was done deliberately and threatened to take the matter to court. The husbands got into the argument and soon the neighborhood

8

was taking sides. I was called in as mediator and finally settled the rose-bush war without litigation.

Our hottest feud lasted almost two years and resulted in some 80 complaints being filed with the police department by a British star of the silent screen and his next-door neighbor, a wealthy restaurateur. The businessman alleged that the actor disturbed the peace by quarreling with his wife and playing the radio full force after hours. Further, he charged, the actor had hurled rocks and obscenities over the hedge at him when he protested. The actor, in turn, complained that his neighbor arrived home noisily every morning at 2 o'clock, driven by a chauffeur who raced the engine, blew the horn, and flashed the headlights of his automobile at the actor's windows. Also, he said, the neighbor's dog howled all night.

In answer to complaints of various neighbors, the actor strung a rope from his back porch to a telephone pole, hung tin cans on it filled with rocks, and yanked it vigorously at intervals, setting up a clamor which could be heard for blocks. He made a dramatic offer to buy all the Pianolas in the vicinity and burn them at a designated spot if his neighbors would sign a pledge to buy no more noise-producing instruments. Later, another actor moved in next-door and the belligerent Briton got into a fuss with him too. The feud ended, finally, in a handshaking and mutual understanding conference in Municipal Court. Eventually the British actor moved away and peace settled on Beverly Hills.

Actors have had more than their share of bad publicity here. Some of it, in cases in which I have known the facts, has been fantastic. The truth is that during my years as a Beverly Hills policeman we have had very little trouble with members of the movie colony. Motion picture people who are successful are no problem. They are too busy to get into mischief. Those who do are usually newcomers unwisely trying to live it up, or former celebrities trying to cling to their fast-fading fame.

Movie stars who used to squander fortunes are more conservative now. Most of them have business agents who put them on a budget and supervise their investments, even limiting their pocket money. The business agents, in turn, have lawyers, accountants and investment advisers, so that a movie or television star's money is more likely to stay with him for a longer period of time. Some stars are among the biggest property-owners in Beverly Hills today. A handsome new office building on Wilshire Boulevard belongs to Alan Ladd; Red Skelton and Fred MacMurray own apartment houses; Joan Crawford, Irene Dunne, Frank Borzage, Jeanette MacDonald and a dozen other celebrities own business property here.

I know actors and actresses whose careers on the screen ended years ago who have become successful business and professional people. One such is Corinne Griffith, who ranks among the city's wealthiest women. Miss Griffith owns all four corners of a choice intersection, with a business building on each corner. In her spare time she writes books. Helen Ferguson, a star of the silent screen, runs a busy publicity agency, and Mary Pickford owns valuable business real estate.

John Barrymore was a constant source of anecdotes during his many years in Beverly Hills, but my only official contact with him was quite unlike any of the stories the public heard. It happened shortly after the Japanese attack on Pearl Harbor when things were pretty nervous in Beverly Hills. With the Pacific Fleet destroyed, and our town just six miles inland from the Pacific Ocean, we felt that we were in the front line of the war. The possibility of an enemy attack was on everyone's mind, and some of us in the police department were on duty 24 hours a day during the early weeks.

One night the phone in my office rang. It was John Barrymore calling, and he wanted to offer his hilltop estate to the government for the duration. "You know, Chief," he said seriously, "it would be a good location for an anti-aircraft battery. The place is built like a fort, and we could drain the swimming pool for a gun emplacement!"

The first two weeks of the war were busy ones for the police department. Since Beverly Hills was in a blackout zone we had to help enforce blackout regulations during several air raid alarms, and also assisted Federal agencies in rounding up enemy aliens and confiscating their firearms, radios and cameras. For a time the basement at headquarters was stacked with equipment taken from these suspects. We also had to enforce the curfew law which required aliens to be off the streets at night.

Our one big night was the false "air raid" in 1942 when all the anti-aircraft guns and searchlights from Santa Monica to Long Beach opened up on an unseen "enemy." The "battle" raged for more than half an hour and hundreds of rounds were fired. From police headquarters, which had been activated as civil defense center, we could see the shellbursts and tracers in the sky overhead. There have been many versions as to just what the target was, with Army and Navy versions differing. The incident was never satisfactorily explained, but one thing was certain, it *looked* and *sounded* authentic.

Although Barrymore's offer was rejected, his action was typical of the movie colony's response to the challenge. Actors and actresses, motion-picture executives and their wives volunteered for duty in the U.S.O., and several actors served as auxiliary officers in our department along with business and professional men. Later, Mary Pickford's estate was used as a week-end recreation center for amputees and paraplegics from nearby military hospitals.

Behind the glamor and glitter of Beverly Hills there is another city which a policeman sees in line of duty, a city of heartbreak for many people. I have known millionaires who died of alcoholism in their mansions, surrounded by servants and luxury; and movie stars who ended up as derelicts. I have known financial men who tried to use their banks and institutions for social advancement, making unsound loans which wrecked their careers and in one case resulted in a prison sentence. I have known too many middle-aged wealthy widows who have been picked off by glib and handsome confidence men, and elderly widowers deceived by unscrupulous women interested only in money. As I write this there is a pretty divorcee with two children who cannot call her fortune

11

her own. She received a huge settlement from her multi-millionaire husband, enough to be independent for life, but she is being kept under wraps by an ex-convict who has taken over as manager of her large home.

A policeman gets to know many characters in a city which attracts unusual people. I remember a solitary Indian woman from Oklahoma who occupied one of our larger residences. I used to see her around the place and assumed she was a domestic, but much to the surprise of a local automobile agency she walked in and ordered two expensive cars. The dealer thought she was crazy until he checked up on her and found she had more money than Carter has pills. She was a ward of the Indian Bureau, loaded with oil royalties. After her cars were delivered she hired a chauffeur, and later married him. However, since there was a suspicion that the driver was more interested in money than romance, the Indian Bureau took steps to safeguard her income. The chauffeur's matrimonial interest waned thereafter and the marriage soon ended.

We had one woman who lived alone in a six-bedroom mansion on a hilltop, with only a maid and caretaker for company. She always wore a veil over her face, never answered the door or spoke to outsiders. When she died she left a substantial sum for the care of her pets. We learned later that she had been jilted in love in her youth and had chosen this way of retiring from life, years before her death.

I remember a distinguished looking retired executive who in his old age acquired a curious hobby. He would wander up and down the alleys collecting discarded articles from rubbish cans and store them in his garage. When he had the garage stuffed from floor to ceiling, a fire inspector accidentally discovered it and ordered the place cleaned out. It took two men and a truck three days to get the job done, and we had to assign a policeman to stand by each day. The old gentleman vigorously opposed the removal of his hoard of junk.

We have people of all kinds in Beverly Hills, misers as

well as philanthropists, and some occasional big spenders like the high-living oil man who enjoyed his dinner so much that he rewarded the blonde waitress with a $1000 tip. The young woman was so overwhelmed that she promptly spent most of the money on a party for her fellow employees.

The sleepy burglar whom we captured under a bed was only one of many unusual criminals who have visited us. We once had a bank robbery staged by a daughter of a millionaire and her playboy husband, who used a borrowed baby as a shield. They were itinerants in Los Angeles who had run out of money. The wife came from a wealthy plantation family in Hawaii, but her husband had nothing except a disdain for honest work. To solve their problem they concocted a novel hold-up. They rented a car and cruised around Beverly Hills until they saw a mother with a 2-year-old son on the street. They stopped to admire the baby and the girl played on the mother's sympathies with a sob story. She had lost her own baby boy, she said, while her husband was away in the service, and it would make them so happy if they could take this beautiful child to the corner drugstore and buy him an ice-cream soda. The mother consented and the couple drove away with the child.

But instead of stopping at the drugstore they went to the nearest bank, where the wife waited in the car while the husband carried the boy inside. With the boy in his arms the husband walked up to a teller's window, handed a surprised teller two stick-up notes, and flourished a gun. A few minutes later he walked out of the bank unchallenged with his tiny hostage and $1200 of the bank's money.

When the couple returned the child to his mother she jotted down the license number of their car, suspicious because they had been gone longer than she had anticipated. After they departed she tried to find out from the boy what had happened, but he was just learning to talk and could say only "Man played cowboy," which meant nothing to her.

Next day, when newspaper headlines reported a bank hold-up in which a small boy had been used as a shield she

13

saw the light and telephoned police headquarters to give us the license number. We soon traced the car to a swank Los Angeles hotel where the couple were registered, checked the description of the man, found it tallied with that of the bank robber, and staked out officers to wait for their return. We arrested them as they parked the car outside the hotel, and discovered they had gone to the racetrack and lost $200 of the bank's money. However, we recovered the rest of the money, jailed the robbers, and wrote off the case as solved in 24 hours.

During Prohibition we had some unusual bootleggers operating in our vicinity. One clever gang of moonshiners took over a private estate on the exclusive "north side" and set up a small distillery. The place was ideal for their purpose, with a large house in front, a stable on the alley at the rear, and all surrounded by shrubbery. Since many residents kept riding horses in those days there was nothing unusual about a truck delivering a load of grain to the stable.

The moonshiners stored their grain and mash in the stable and converted two bedrooms in the house into a still, with wooden vats reaching from floor to ceiling. An elaborate blower system forced the fumes from their operation down into the sewer system to prevent alcoholic aromas from floating across the neighborhood. They concealed the large amount of gas used in their "cooking" by simply by-passing the gas meter, an illegal maneuver which also saved them money. Everything looked normal on the premises. A family occupied the front of the house and a gardener kept the grounds beautifully. But all this enterprise went down the drain when Federal agents and local police raided the place after it had been going about two months.

I shut off another source of supply one night when I encountered a college student weaving out of an apartment-house carrying two bottles of bootleg liquor and an alcoholic breath. It wasn't too difficult to find out where he got the stuff. "Second floor, last apartment back. Ring the buzzer and ask 'Is Mabel in?'" he confided. I followed directions and was welcomed into a large apartment by a gorgeous blonde who wanted to know whether I preferred Scotch, bourbon or gin. I confessed I didn't drink and was there only for the purpose of arresting the occupants. She let out a startled yelp and headed for the bathroom, with me at her heels. Inside the bathroom was her husband, busily stirring a tub full of freshly-made gin.

Inspecting the apartment later we found it set up for large-scale bootlegging. The closet was filled with bottles, labels, whiskey coloring and other supplies. One item which amused me was a spray gun filled with salt water, for customers who demanded liquor "right off the boat." The bootleggers sprayed salt water on the burlap which they wrapped around their bottles of home-made "Scotch" and got fantastic prices for this "imported stuff."

All sorts of ruses were used for distribution of bootleg booze. Milkmen sometimes left it on doorsteps in bottles painted white, several grocery drivers concealed bottles among the groceries they delivered at homes, and at least one bottled-water salesman carried it in his truck as a sideline. Presumably he sold the five gallon bottles of water as a chaser. Tony Cornero and other rum-runners were operating along the coast, unloading liquor from foreign ships at Malibu, Paradise Cove and other sheltered spots on Santa Monica Bay.

In a later chapter, I will get to the jewel thieves and burglars, some of them internationally known, who have "hit" Beverly Hills during the years, but we've also had some ingenious local fellows whose unique methods have kept them fresh in my memory. One crafty burglar, a seafaring man and caretaker on a yacht, carried a small acetylene torch on his shoulder like a knapsack and a coil of rope attached to a steel hook. When he visited Beverly Hills he stood in an alley behind a store building, tossed the hook to the roof where it caught and held, then climbed the rope hand over hand and pulled it up after him, leaving no evidence for a passing patrolman that a burglar was at work. He cut a hole in the roof, but failed to notice several small wires which he touched. These set off a silent burglar alarm and he soon found himself surrounded by police.

A small, inoffensive looking ex-convict who carried a violin case under his arm almost fooled us once. Anybody seeing him on the street would take him for a musician, but inside the case he had a sawed-off shotgun and a sledge hammer. Our radio patrol officers caught him one night when he was pounding away at the knob on a market safe. He fired the shotgun at one officer, spraying him with buckshot, but was captured before he could do more damage.

Another burglar, fleeing from a house where an officer had surprised him, vanished into the ground like a gopher. He had dropped into a large storm drain which runs under the city to carry off winter rainfall. We called out all cars to watch the many outlets of the drain, and were waiting patiently for him when he came to the surface a mile away.

I remember a crooked jewelry salesman who took jewels on consignment from individuals who advertised them for sale, and later claimed he had lost them. His stories were dramatic. Once, he said, he was kidnapped and robbed. Another time he reported he had lost a large diamond down a toilet in a Los Angeles hotel, and on a third occasion he claimed he had been held-up in Hollywood. We disproved all his stories and had him in jail, awaiting trial, when we got another "break" in the case. He had secretly dispatched a woman social worker from the jail to dig up a can which he had buried in his father-in-law's yard without the latter's knowledge. When the father-in-law saw a strange woman digging surreptitiously in his yard he called the police, and we recovered the can of "lost" jewelry and assured the culprit's extended stay in prison.

Another odd "customer" we handled was the son of a wealthy family who had dissipated his fortune but had managed to make a small name for himself as a writer of motion-picture and television scripts. Because he knew many people he was able to write bad checks for thousands of dollars in various cities throughout California, victimizing the friends who had known him when he had money. He was married several times, and we caught up with him just after he had bought his latest wife some expensive gifts, with worthless checks.

The glamorous surroundings of Beverly Hills do not make police work any less dangerous here than it is anywhere else. We have lost several fine officers who gave their lives in line of duty. In one case I remember vividly Detective Walt Grider was bringing a burglary suspect to headquarters at night for interrogation. He had received a "rumble" on the suspect, but not enough information to justify handcuffing him. The man was sitting beside Grider in the front seat of a police car. When the car slowed down for an intersection he leaped out and started running. Grider ran after him in the darkness, following him into the back yard of a nearby residence. The owner of the house, hearing the disturbance outside, armed himself with a .22 caliber revolver and stepped to the door to investigate. As he opened the door the suspect yelled: "There's a guy trying to hold me up!" Before Grider could identify himself the homeowner fired one shot which struck him in the heart, killing him almost instantly. As he fell, however, he shot and wounded the suspect seriously.

When I arrived I found Walt Grider lying dead on the driveway, and the burglary suspect paralyzed and moaning in the back yard. The homeowner was grievously shocked when he learned he had killed a police officer instead of a hold-up man, but it was too late to reverse his fateful mistake. It was also too late for Detective Grider to know he had done his duty well. The man he had been bringing in was guilty of burglary; I found the evidence in the suspect's pockets.

two

CLARA BOW'S

MIDNIGHT VISITOR

WHEN I BEGAN AS A PATROLMAN 30 YEARS AGO, VACANT lots outnumbered buildings on Wilshire Boulevard, and undeveloped tracts separated Beverly Hills from the surrounding Los Angeles suburbs, which have since built up solidly to our borders.

The city was having growing pains. Planned as an estate community, with lovely homes, large estates and seven miles of bridle paths, it had many citizens who wanted to keep it this way. But population and business were moving in on all sides. I can remember a civic battle over whether the city should permit a dime store to locate in the shopping district. And to prevent business from encroaching on its north-side homes, the city spent more than $600,000 buying and landscaping a two-mile strip of parkway along Santa Monica Boulevard, which now permanently keeps the residential and shopping areas a discreet distance apart.

Police work was primitive by today's standards. Our police vehicles were open touring cars, Fords or Chevrolets, and bicycles. When the winter rains came—and it sometimes pours in Southern California—the cars had leaky side-curtains which didn't offer much protection from the weather. It was almost as comfortable on a bike then.

We used bikes on some of the beats. Bicycles were not bad going downhill, but the uphill trip was tough pumping. Besides which, my six-foot, 200-pound frame didn't seem to be naturally fitted to this form of transportation. One embarrassment in the daily lives of bicycle policemen was that the city's young "hot-rodders" knew we couldn't catch them. They would whiz past in their cut-down Model-T's and "give us the bird." We had to suffer in silence and maintain official dignity by ignoring the juvenile jeers.

However, riding a bike for eight hours a day kept me physically fit, and on days off I further sharpened my condition by working out with wrestlers on the beach at Santa Monica. Physical fitness is essential in police work; I still keep in shape by working out three days a week at the athletic club, lifting weights, punching the bag and swimming.

Instead of modern mobile radio communications we had red and green lights installed at high points throughout the city. One set of lights was on a watertower near the present location of the City Hall. Patrolmen on duty were supposed to keep one eye on their beat and the other on the lights, which usually hung from convenient utility poles. In addition we had to check in every half-hour from one of the police call boxes located at many points in the city. When a red light glowed, all uniform men hurried to the nearest call box and reported to the office. The green bulb notified all detectives and officers to check in. And when both red and green lights came on it was an emergency calling for every man.

As policemen we were also supposed to know how to run the city's ambulance, an elderly vehicle, and often when we answered the red light it would be a summons to act as driver. We had a small emergency hospital under Dr. Charles F. Nelson, a private physician, who would hurry over from his home or office when needed. I can still remember driving that old Cadillac on an emergency call on dark nights. Whenever anyone blew the siren on the ambulance its headlights went dim, so the object at nighttime was to get to your destination as fast as possible without blowing the siren too much. And in a pinch it was difficult to decide whether the noise or the headlights would be more effective.

Late one night years ago when I was on duty, the red lights on the waterfront flashed on, and I pulled up at the nearest call box.

"Anderson reporting, what's up?"

"We've just had a call from Clara Bow's home in the 500 block on North Roxbury Drive." I mentally placed the location eight or nine blocks away as the Sergeant continued. "Some guy's pounding down the front door, may be a drunk. Go take a look."

I roared off in my four-cylinder Chevy and arrived to find a giant of a man trying to get in the front door of Miss Bow's palatial mansion. As I came up behind him, he seemed to be attempting to talk to someone through the peephole. I'm no midget, but he towered over me and had the longest arms I'd ever seen.

"Look mister," I said, trying to place myself between him and the door, "what's this all about? What are you doing here at this time of night? Do you know whose house this is?"

He seemed annoyed by the interruption and said to me with some pride, "Of course I know whose house it is. It belongs to Miss Bow. And I came out here all the way from Iowa to propose marriage to Miss Bow, only she won't open the door."

He brushed me aside and began pounding his big paw on the door again. His goal of making Miss Bow his bride stirred a tiny amount of sympathy under my blue uniform, because at this time Clara Bow was the dream girl of almost every red-blooded man alive; she was, of course, the Marilyn Monroe-Bridgitte Bardot of that day.

Honorable though his intentions might have been, it soon became apparent that Miss Bow's corn-fed caller was off his rocker. I braced myself and began the ancient ritual familiar to every policeman of trying to send the troublemaker on his way and restore peace and order to his beat. Big Boy was diverted momentarily and showed me the title to his farm in Iowa, which he was about to lay at the feet of his goddess. He seemed a trifle hurt by the cool reception he was getting in Beverly Hills. "Where I come from, boy," he complained, "when anybody comes to the door and knocks, why we invite them inside. Now how about getting me in to talk to Miss Bow there?"

I talked through the peephole to a frightened young woman who identified herself as Miss Bow's secretary. Miss Bow, it seemed, had prudently retreated when it was obvious that her Romeo was going to be hard to discourage. The man had been pounding on the door for some time she said, and refused to leave. At that, I made up my mind. Since he was obviously disturbing the peace and conducting himself in a disorderly manner, I turned to face this giant and attempted to slip handcuffs on him as quickly as possible. To my dismay and Romeo's amusement, his wrists were so thick I could not close the handcuffs around them. Only momentarily chagrined, I began easing and guiding him down the front drive to my patrol car. I somehow convinced him that he'd better pursue his romance at a more convenient hour. I guess he finally got it into his head that I might intercede in his behalf and thus got him to headquarters without much further trouble except for a running commentary on the wedded bliss he envisioned with Miss Bow.

Looking back on it now, I see I'd have been much better off escorting him to the city limits than hauling my huge catch up to the desk for booking. We all agreed that for his own safekeeping and the peace of North Roxbury Drive, our Iowa visitor should spend the night as our guest. I looked in on him just before going off my shift, and he was still going on about his plans to renew the romance with my help and perhaps just beginning to perceive that he was, after all, locked up tight for the night.

Next morning, when I called at the jail to check on my guest's condition, I found he had wreaked havoc in the place. Enormously strong, he had pulled out the plumbing in his cell, broken off the water pipes and flooded the entire jail. The Sergeant cautioned me to stay out of Big Boy's sight since we didn't want the whole building shaken down. He was speedily turned over to other authorities for mental examination, and a small squad of orderlies arrived to take him off our hands. Shortly thereafter, he was on his way home as a mental case.

We had Prohibition in those days, and nobody was supposed to get drunk, but somehow they did. When a walking patrolman picked up a drunk he had to wrestle him to the jail on foot, sometimes as much as half a mile through the business district, or subdue him and put him in a patrol car if one was available. My particular burden was a fellow who was part Indian and played the role of the village drunk. I arrested him numerous times, and on each occasion I had to scuffle with him all the way to the jail, dodging his wild blows and holding him upright. We finally got rid of him. The judge, tired of continually sentencing him to short "drying-out" periods, gave him a really stiff sentence which apparently discouraged him. He moved away afterwards and gave his patronage to other jails.

But patrolling also had its pleasant side. Often as I rode a bike along Rodeo Drive on a summer morning I would see Hobart Bosworth, the distinguished actor, white-haired and erect, riding a handsome horse on the bridle path. Sometimes I would stop to chat with Ben Turpin, the cross-eyed comedian of the silent movies, who loved to visit with the neighborhood patrolman; or wave a greeting to Buster Keaton, or Monte Blue, or Tom Mix, all famous residents of Beverly Hills.

I met Will Rogers, the cowboy humorist and actor, on many occasions, but one stands out in my mind. I was walking my beat on Santa Monica Boulevard when a car came around the corner, turning too close to the curb. The rear

22

wheel jolted over the curb and down with a violent bounce. The driver stopped to inspect the possible damage. It was Will Rogers. "Well, if I'd been on a horse I'd 'a made it!," he said, grinning.

Will and his family lived in a large house on Beverly Drive, and I remember his two sons as small but inquisitive youngsters whom we occasionally shooed away when they stopped at the jail, out of curiosity, hoping to look at the prisoners. Will, Junior, has since been Congressman, newspaper publisher and actor, and Jimmy Rogers a successful rancher. During the depression we used to see Model-T jalopies with Oklahoma license plates heading toward Will's house for handouts. He was considered a big man there as well as here.

Will Rogers did more than anyone else to put Beverly Hills on the map. He datelined his syndicated daily newspaper columns from here, and quipped about the city on the radio and in his many films. When he returned from a cross-country trip in 1926 his fellow citizens organized a posse, met him at the train in Los Angeles, and took him to a platform erected near the Beverly Hills Hotel for a ceremony proclaiming him honorary "Mayor of Beverly Hills." He got a lot of fun out of the title; and we got nationwide publicity. His letter to Andrew Mellon, Secretary of the Treasury, in 1929, requesting a new Post Office building for the city, was instrumental in developing our Civic Center, although we had to wait until FDR's first term for the Post Office.

Will's tragic death in an airplane crash in Alaska with Wiley Post, in 1935, while they were on a flight to the Orient, was felt as a personal loss by the citizens of his favorite city. His name lives on in Will Rogers Memorial Park and in a children's drinking fountain in Roxbury Park.

Beverly Hills went through some hard times after the stock market crash in 1929. I was walking a beat in the business district during the depression that followed, and remember the day a bank closed its doors. Many homes were for sale; mansions on the exclusive "north side" went begging

23

at prices as low as $20,000. A real-estate man, two stock brokers and a banker took the suicide route out of their financial troubles. One suicide seemed particularly senseless: A man and his wife who had lost several millions, but had other millions left, decided they could not endure it any longer and ended their lives by taking poison.

One citizen who had been worth several hundred thousand dollars lost it all, and got a job on the police force. Police jobs were hard to get then, because nobody quit. However, our once-wealthy policeman could not adjust to living on a lower scale. He tried to increase his income and was dismissed, to try other lines of work.

We could count on regular winter visitors at the City Jail, as vagrants from all over the United States came here for shelter from the cold. They cleverly arranged to be picked up for vagrancy in California in winter, and in Connecticut and northeastern States in the summer, which seemed like careful, prudent planning, worthy of a more serious purpose.

During the depression years I was dispatched to a beautiful and imposing mansion with a warrant from Huntington Beach, Calif., to pick up an oil man who had failed to pay his workers. As I rang the bell at the massive front door, my subject ran out the back door and attempted to get away in a car parked in the driveway. As he did so, I jumped on the running board and pinned his arms at his sides, forcing him to stop. Then I handcuffed him for a ride to the station.

At the time I weighed over 200 pounds and was working out regularly with the beach wrestlers. My prisoner, however, was so soft physically that his arms were black and blue where I had grabbed him. Later he complained to the City Council that I had not treated him like a gentleman. My answer was that no gentleman would resist or attempt to escape a police officer on duty. We investigated this gentleman and found he was a shady oil promoter who owed everybody in town. His large home was a false front with a huge mortgage on it. It was a lesson for me in values, and imparted this knowledge I've seen verified often in Beverly Hills: An individual who drives a big car and lives in a mansion doesn't necessarily own either one of them.

It has not often been necessary for me to use physical force in making an arrest. I have always kept in good shape through exercise, and if an average individual senses you are physically fit and can handle yourself, he will not resist. Professional criminals seldom offer any resistance when nabbed. The only ones who are unpredictable are panicky teen-agers, dope addicts and drunks.

I suppose most of the individuals I have had to arrest disliked me intensely when it happened, or even hated me. But frequently on my visits to State prisons I meet prisoners who I sent to the penitentiary and am greeted with a cheerful, "Hello there, Mr. Anderson. How's everything in Beverly Hills?" Most criminals will do everything in their power to beat the charges against them, but once they are in prison they realize the policeman who put them there was only doing his duty.

The police department took a long step forward in 1936 when two-way radio equipment was installed on police motorcycles. It was the first such installation in the United States, engineered by a radio technician, Faust Gonset, who is now a leading electronics manufacturer. A year later we had the radio system on our patrol cars also, but the early-day headaches with our communications equipment were sometimes perplexing.

The city's lovely canyons and curving streets were an obstacle to police radio communications. In the canyons, patrol cars could neither receive nor send messages until relay booster stations were built on hilltops and office buildings. Then doctors discovered diathermy, and we couldn't operate in the business district until a way was found to quiet the doctors' machines. Even the streetcars on Santa Monica Boulevard were a problem until they were replaced by busses.

The copper dome of our handsome City Hall was found to be interfering with our system. Our police calls were frequently getting mixed up with calls from half a dozen eastern cities which had radios on the same wave-length. One winter day, Officer Harnage, cruising along amid flowers and sunshine, heard his number called on the radiophone: "Calling Car Two. Go to Twenty-sixth and Parkway and stop children from sliding downhill on ice. That is all." Since the temperature was 80 degrees and there was no snow, Harnage knew the call was not for him. Later he learned it was from the Newark, N.J., police department. A new remote tower helped solve this problem, but even today we occasionally get our wireless crossed with other cities.

I remember a prowler call in the 600 block on North Bedford Drive when I was a uniform officer. A housewife in a large home surrounded by extensive grounds called the police when she heard a suspicious noise in the yard. At the same time, without telling us, she let out the family watchdog, a huge German Shepherd, to hunt the intruder. As I walked through the shrubbery, swinging a flashlight, this dog suddenly came around the corner of the house at top speed and went for me. He grabbed my leg in his viselike teeth, while I called for help from the house. Luckily, I was wearing black leather leggings, which were part of our uniform then, and escaped injury. If there was a prowler in that yard, the dog had either eaten him or scared him off before I got there.

One Sunday at daybreak, I saw a youth who looked like a college student walking down one of our main streets with a twenty-foot length of two-by-four lumber on his shoulder, and a telephone book under his shirt. He explained it was all part of a fraternity initiation, and that he had to steal these two things and report back to the house. I reported along with him and discovered a treasure room of red lanterns, No Parking signs, traffic lane markers, and other items of city property, which were promptly returned.

One local resident is immensely proud of a large cast-iron statue of a St. Bernard dog which stands on a cement slab on his front lawn. It must weigh a ton or more, but periodically it is upset by pranksters, and sometimes we find they are fraternity initiatees.

Motion picture stars were more noticeable in Beverly Hills in the 1930's than today. Sometimes almost half of the diners at the local Brown Derby would be film celebrities. Since then they have been partially displaced by the businessmen, lawyers, stock brokers, oil men and industrialists of this booming city.

Estates were larger and more numerous in the old days, too. I can remember answering a prowler call at the home of Gloria Swanson, who lived on a huge estate across the street from the Beverly Hills Hotel. It took half an hour just to cover the grounds, and we found nobody. This place has since been subdivided, as have many others, and has three large modern homes on it. The old Charlie Chapin estate on Summit Drive is now the site of several new homes, and the scenic 402-acre Doheny Ranch, where early-morning patrolmen used to see deer feeding, has been subdivided into 500 homesites, some of them selling for at least $100,000 each.

Clara Bow's uninvited "boy friend" was only one of many ardent movie fans who have visited us during the years. I remember a plumber from Chicago who flew into town to ask for the hand of Sylvia Sidney. He had copies of love letters he had written her (unanswered), and a couple of hundred dollars with which he proposed to set up housekeeping with Miss Sidney. He was persuaded to return home unmarried. A cab driver from Philadelphia drove all the way to Beverly Hills to propose to Jean Harlow, about a year after that dazzling platinum blonde star had died. He came to police headquarters to locate her, and we had a time convincing him she was dead, but he finally gave up and went home.

Lovestruck swains, and occasionally women, arrive here every year with marriage offers for movie and television stars, but most of them are persuaded to go home without the intervention of the police department. I sometimes wonder

27

if the re-runs of old movies showing the glamor queens of 30 years ago on television will bring us a new influx of starry-eyed suitors. And how about those old Clara Bow movies!

Working conditions in the police department have changed since my patrol and detective days. Oldtime policemen faced more hardships than today's officers. They were in better physical condition because they walked, or rode bikes, instead of sitting in automobiles. And there was less absenteeism. All of the men who were on the force when I began have either retired, quit or passed away. Some of them have become chiefs and police executives in other cities, or head security forces in industries.

We were far removed from today's modern equipment and methods. We had to write our own reports on the typewriter, for example, and the fact that none of us was an expert typist made no difference. Officers today dictate their reports to a stenographer. They also have the services of a modern crime laboratory with photographic, recording and detection equipment; teletype connections with State and County crime information lines; a record file with tens of thousands of fingerprint cards and other criminal data; a Stevenson Breathalyser for use in drunk arrests; a small but complete armory with rifles, shotguns, tear-gas guns and armored vests; and a unique "line-up" room where suspects on the stage are viewed under colored lights which can simulate morning, noon, sunset or street light illumination for the benefit of witnesses. (Viewing is done through a one-way mirrored wall to protect the security of the witnesses.)

Anyone who wants a clock-watching job should not be a policeman. The day's work is never done for a good officer. He has to be willing to work unusual and irregular hours. There is too much tendency in all lines of work now to put in eight hours on the job, and then forget it. In police work, however, there are certain functions that do not follow a mechanical routine. If you are a detective interrogating a suspect you have to keep at it until you find out how the

28

fellow's mind is operating. You can't just knock off at 5 P.M. and turn him over to others for questioning. It used to be a personal challenge to a detective if he thought a criminal was putting something over on him, and he would go without sleep, if necessary, to solve a case.

Police work is not glamorous. It is a matter of sheer perseverance rather than brilliant deduction. Much of it is dull routine, so that discipline has to be maintained to keep a department operating at top efficiency. Discipline requires constant supervision of personnel and a semi-military organization.

Through the years this policy has been followed in Beverly Hills. Proof of its success is demonstrated, I believe, by the fact that during my term as Chief of Police the city has had nine different Mayors. This is a rather unusual record when one considers the fast turnover of police chiefs in other American cities.

three

HOW PATROLS

CATCH CROOKS

ONE OF JACK BENNY'S FUNNIEST TELEVISION SHOWS WAS his takeoff on the Beverly Hills Police Department in which he pictured our headquarters as a showplace with period furniture, wall-to-wall carpeting, crystal chandeliers, a beautiful blonde receptionist, and an unlisted telephone. (We didn't want just *anybody* calling!) Business was by appointment only, and when Mr. Benny arrived, without an appointment, to report his Maxwell stolen we were horrified; we wouldn't stir out of the office for anything smaller than a Cadillac. Our police radio system offered rich background music between calls, and our police dogs, naturally, were French poodles!

The police department enjoyed this lampoon as much as the public. Previously our most memorable official contact with Mr. Benny, a longtime resident of Beverly Hills, had occurred when a new maid at his home on North Roxbury Drive pushed the button on the silent burglar alarm by mistake, bringing down two police cars on the surprised comedian in a very few minutes.

Amusing as this episode was, it demonstrated one phase of the elaborate system of police protection we have developed for this wealthy community. Our modus operandi has received considerable national publicity through the years. And while we are proud of this recognition, we do not claim our methods are superior to police procedure in other cities. What works in Beverly Hills might not be necessary elsewhere, since each community has its own special problems.

Our basic idea resembles the old Chinese medical plan in which the doctor is paid to keep the patient well, not to cure him after he gets sick. Citizens of Beverly Hills pay their police department to keep crime away from the city. Our purpose is the prevention and detection of crime, rather than boasting of the number of catches we make. We have a modern department organized in four divisions, Patrol, Traffic, Detective, Records and Communications, with well-trained patrol officers and detectives, a fine crime laboratory, a spotless jail and an up-to-date communications system.

The core of our plan is a motor patrol which operates around the clock, keeping watch on the city's streets 24 hours a day. Patrol cars, equipped with three-way radio and in constant communication with headquarters, travel all of the streets within the city at frequent intervals. They are conspicuously marked in black-and-white so that both the public and potential evildoers are aware of their presence. Nothing discourages criminals more than the knowledge that a police car is only two minutes away—the average time needed for a Beverly Hills patrol car to reach any point in its district after receiving a call. To prevent lawbreakers from knowing their exact location at any given time, the cars follow an unpredictable pattern of movement, frequently backtracking.

Since criminals and hoodlums rarely strike unless given a good opportunity, constant surveillance is an effective deterrent to crime. Our police records show that motor patrol officers have often caught criminals preparing to commit an offense, or in the act, and sometimes have apprehended them before the victims are aware a crime has been committed.

Two burglars, using a panel truck disguised as a cleaner's

delivery wagon, were busily removing expensive suits from a haberdashery when a police car, summoned by a silent alarm, rolled up and took them into custody. Two seafaring men, one of them formerly employed by a motion-picture star, hauled themselves and a canvas bag of tools to the roof of a building by means of a rope with a hook on the end, cut a hole in the roof, and were working on a safe in the store below when a patrol car arrived. One market burglar was caught with his hand in an open cash register. A man and two women, who tossed a concrete block through the window of a jewelry store at 3 A.M. and took handfuls of watches and gems, were nabbed by patrol officers just as they were getting into an automobile to leave the scene.

I recall one arrest which had a typical hometown flavor. A patrol officer came upon two men leaving a large home in broad daylight, carrying bundles wrapped in bed sheets. The men explained they had just rented the house and were taking some things to the laundry. Their story seemed plausible but the officer was still suspicious. "How much rent do you have to pay for a place like this?," he asked casually. "One hundred dollars a month," was the answer. The officer put them under arrest immediately. He knew a Beverly Hills home of this size rented for five or six times this figure. Opening the bundles, he found them filled with clothing and valuables belonging to Sy Bartlett, a well-known screen writer, who lived in the house.

The grand ball at the gala opening of the Beverly Hilton Hotel attracted a glittering crowd of celebrities. As the guests were departing, two officers on patrol noticed some suspicious characters in a parked car, and gave chase when the car attempted a quick getaway. They overtook the suspects a short distance away and forced them to the curb. Inside the car the officers found three ex-convicts, two revolvers, and $20,000 worth of stolen furs and jewelry. The gunmen had followed two guests to a home in an adjacent community, robbed them of money, gems and furs as they drove into a garage, and returned to the hotel to wait for other victims. The fast action of the patrol officers recovered the stolen property before a report on it was received from the neighboring city.

Three 18-year-old youths who parked their automobile near a boulevard "stop" late at night were investigated by patrol officers who found three firearms in the car. After their arrest the three youths confessed that they had planned to hold up the first Cadillac which halted at the "stop" sign. They were confident that anyone driving such an expensive car would be a top prospect for a stick-up.

Because of our constant patrolling it is almost impossible for prostitution and gambling to flourish here. Patrol officers are quickly aware of any sudden increase in the number of cars parked in front of a residence or apartment, and the traffic in and out of the place. For the same reason, very little scandal develops in Beverly Hills. If anything sinful is going on, the Chief of Police is likely to be one of the first to know!

When the operatives of *Confidential* headquartered here and set up pipelines to gather scandal items on Hollywood celebrities for the magazine, police were soon aware of their activities. Patrol officers began to wonder why private detectives were making so many visits to a certain address, and nobody is more curious than an inquisitive policeman. Later, of course, *Confidential* switched to a less hazardous field of interest and several motion-picture personalities breathed easier.

The close watch we keep over our streets, particularly after nightfall, has occasionally caused ruffled tempers when pedestrians in quiet residential districts have been stopped for questioning by patrol officers. I remember one incident (I can see the humor in it *now*) involving a new officer who stopped a "suspicious character" and asked the man to identify himself. It was a former mayor of our city, out for a late evening stroll in his old clothes.

There is a local joke that anyone walking our streets after dark must be accompanied by a dog to avert suspicion. This is not true. Several ingenious prowlers have tried strolling dogs near the scene of a contemplated crime, but they were intercepted because they showed more interest in the homes they were "casing" than in their canine companions. And one wag observed that our patrol officers even know the *dogs* in their districts.

Stationary automobiles with people in them are closely scrutinized by patrol cars, and neckers are politely shooed away because this activity has often been used as a cover-up by burglars. The housebreaker leaves a woman in a car parked outside the house as a lookout; when a police car approaches, the woman sounds the horn and the burglar quickly leaves the house and gets into the car where the couple pretend to be necking. On one occasion a patrol officer came upon a parked car with a woman in it who said she had become ill while driving and had stopped to rest. She assured the officer she would be all right in a few minutes, and be on her way. The officer drove on down the street, but kept the car under observation. Minutes later a man walked out of a house carrying a suitcase and got in the car. The officer doubled back and caught a burglar with a suitcase full of loot.

Private citizens who go out of town on business trips or vacations, leaving their homes vacant and unguarded, can advise patrol officers of their absence, and their homes will be checked for security at various intervals every day while they are away.

A silent burglar alarm system has protected many of the city's wealthier homes for many years. Originally it was operated by the police department. For a nominal fee householders could have concealed buttons, door alarms and burglar beams wired directly to headquarters. Then, if a motion-picture celebrity's home was threatened, a push of a button would summon the police.

There were some mishaps with the early system, as when a happy party guest would get fouled up in the wiring and summon police to a party to which they had not been invited. One embarrassed subscriber arrived home from a two-weeks hunting trip, in whiskers and old clothes, and let himself in the back door of his home, forgetting that the alarm system was still on. He was fixing himself a snack in the kitchen when the police arrived. Because of his unkempt appearance,

34

and the fact that he was carrying a knife and gun, he had to talk fast to prove his identity. He finally woke up his wife, who was sleeping upstairs, to identify him.

As the city grew and more requests for silent alarms were made, the system was sold to a commercial concern which now relays signals immediately to police headquarters when an alarm button is pushed. One apprehensive picture personality has buttons for the alarm in every room, including the bathrooms, where hold-up men frequently lock victims. Other householders have buttons by doors, beds and windows.

When a burglar alarm signal reaches police headquarters, two cars go directly to the house, one to the front and one to the rear. Two more cars block off the immediate area. If a criminal is not picked up at the scene of the crime, the chances are that he will soon be flushed in the vicinity. Recently burglars broke into the fur vault of a well-wired mansion, whose owners had left it vacant while they vacationed in Palm Springs. Summoned by the silent alarm, patrol cars converged on the house within two minutes after getting the signal, and caught the looters in the vault with thousands of dollars worth of furs in their arms.

One of the local banks became suspicious of two men who had entered and left the bank several times during the day without transacting any noticeable amount of business. When both men re-entered the bank just before closing time, the manager used the silent alarm system to call for police assistance. Officers quickly arrived. They questioned the suspects, one of whom was armed, and determined the men had come to Beverly Hills from another city for the purpose of robbing the bank. The men were booked on suspicion at the City Jail, and later one of them confessed to their intentions and implicated the other.

A unique feature in the department's arrest record is that more than 98 per cent of the felony arrests we make every year are of individuals living outside the city limits who have entered Beverly Hills for the purpose of committing a crime.

Frequently these uninvited guests will use various disguises in an attempt to avoid detection. Early-morning and week-end burglars who hit commercial buildings favor janitor apparel, sometimes placing brooms and other equipment in their cars to make it appear they are there for the purpose of cleaning up the premises. This disguise hasn't been too successful, however, because our patrol officers make it their business to know the regular janitors.

In this connection, we have recently noticed a change in the pattern of such burglaries, the result of economic changes in building-management. Buildings which formerly employed their own janitor now frequently turn this work over to janitor services with numerous employees, who sometimes quit their jobs after accumulating keys to several buildings and return to loot the offices they once cleaned.

Western Union, cab-driver and chauffeur uniforms are also popular disguises, and some criminals arrive at "work" dressed as gardeners (in pick-up trucks), or as electricians, plumbers, telephone men and meter-readers. Often their women confederates will be dressed as maids and nurses to cover up their real identities. However, they seldom deceive patrol officers who, because of the smallness of our patrol districts, can spot strangers in the area on sight.

Beverly Hills police officers are hand-picked. They are required to attend in-service training courses regularly, receive Ju-jitsu training in self-defense classes, keep physically fit in gymnasium sessions, and meet minimum requirements on the police pistol range, a soundproof indoor range built beneath the city shops building.

Defendants fight to get in our City Jail, a model of neatness and security, which has been commended many times by the Los Angeles County Grand Jury as the cleanest jail in the county. We have had several famous "names" behind the bars, but not many; and two men whom I jailed years ago on bad check charges are now successful business men and community leaders.

Through the years in City Jail we have had some unusual prisoners, like the two wealthy citizens who were victims of John Barleycorn and were arrested repeatedly on drunk charges. The judge finally sentenced them to three-to-six

36

months each in an attempt to straighten them out. They both had incomes of between $3000 and $4000 a month, and on the first and 15th day of the month their families would come to the jail with handfuls of checks to be signed. One millionaire "client" was the best trusty we ever had. He painted the jail, kept the floors polished, washed police cars, and made himself generally useful around the station. Few of the bums doing time in jail for vagrancy knew that the trusty who served them their meals was a wealthy man.

Probably the toughest prisoners we ever had in jail were three young gunmen from Dillinger territory in Indiana, aged 20 to 25 years. With two other confederates they had pulled hold-ups in Indianapolis, Terre Haute, South Bend, and Los Angeles. Early one morning, at 5:30 A.M., the daring quintet hit the exclusive Beverly Hills Hotel. They forced the night manager at gunpoint to open the safe, and made off with a sizeable amount of money and jewelry belonging to guests. They were spotted by a radio patrol car when they stopped to change stolen cars about a mile from the hotel, and opened fire on the approaching police car. Police returned their fire and captured three of the gang, recovering the jewels and the money.

In City Jail, the trio assaulted Jailer H. R. Niestrum when he went to feed them lunch, then ran down a corridor and jumped from a third-story window to a tall palm tree outside. We quickly rounded them up, after they shinnied down the palm tree, and returned them to jail, this time in separate cells. They were convicted and sent to State prison at San Quentin where, later, two of them escaped to the East, pulling a series of hold-ups on their way. Captured in Mississippi, the pair escaped again, and were finally recaptured in Memphis, Tenn. All three in this gang were daredevils without brains, robbing for thrills. Always armed and ready to shoot without cause, they were more dangerous than any professional.

Because of the social and economic status of Beverly Hills, the police department on occasion has been subjected to attacks by left-wing political groups, who like to imply that "favoritism" rather than law enforcement is practiced here. However, the ordinances and regulations we have in Beverly Hills are essential because of the concentration of wealth. In some cities, one or two prominent citizens may carry the weight in the community and "run the town." In Beverly Hills a large percentage of our citizens are influential in many fields—banking, politics, commerce, industry, entertainment and others. The police department cannot play favorites. If the irate fellow complaining to the police about barking dogs keeping him awake is a millionaire, the man who owns the dogs is very probably also a millionaire. As far as "influence" goes, it is a stand-off. We have one citizen who cannot resist turning in false fire alarms whenever he has a few drinks, and he goes to jail every time. He is the son of a New York banker, with an income of $3500 a month.

What our detractors never mention is that wealthy and prominent people who become involved with the law usually are punished more severely than an average citizen because of the unfavorable publicity they receive. Nobody gets too excited when John Doe lands in jail, but when it happens to a celebrity or prominent citizen the man is pilloried. And often, because of his prominence, he is given a stiffer sentence than he otherwise would get, as well as the publicity.

Our police department, enforcing the law without fear or favor, also makes friends for Beverly Hills. When James A. FitzPatrick, nationally-known writer and producer of motion-picture travelogues, moved to Palm Springs after 20 years residence in Beverly Hills, he wrote a letter of thanks to former Mayor George W. Davis in appreciation of many privileges enjoyed as a resident of the city. "First of all," he wrote, "we are extremely grateful for the very efficient protection and service which we have received from the Beverly Hills police force. . . . As a matter of fact, in the many years that I have devoted to world travel I have not found anywhere a police department that could excel that of Beverly Hills."

How many other cities, I wonder, get fan mail like this from satisfied citizens?

four

ALMOST

A HERO

YEARS AGO, WHEN I WAS NEW ON THE FORCE, AN EXCITED
housewife on Crescent Drive called to report she had just
seen a man under a window of the house next door. "Hurry!
He's still there!," she added. I headed for the scene in a
police car at top speed, hoping to make a fast catch of a
burglar. It was 11 P.M. and dark enough for burglary.

The woman who had turned in the report was waiting
on the sidewalk, about 100 feet from the house in question.
As she was telling me what she had seen, a dim figure came
out of the window, caught sight of us, and quickly crouched
down behind a hedge. I advanced toward the spot, but had
taken only a few steps when a man jumped out and sprinted
up the street away from me. I yelled for him to stop, and
fired in the air, but he kept going at top speed. I gave chase
and saw him run inside a house which was under construction. Following him in, I found him hiding in a corner. He
had no shoes on. I handcuffed him and led him to the
police car.

But I soon discovered that my "burglar" was only a badly

frightened college student, who had been carrying on an affair with a married woman. He admitted that on several occasions he had crept into and out of the house after the rather elderly man of the house had retired for the night. It just happened that tonight a neighbor had observed him. He had parked his car a block away with his shoes in it. I locked him up for the night. Next morning I went back to verify his story with the lady of the house, waiting discreetly until after her husband had left for work.

This surprise conclusion to my burglar chase was disappointing to me. I had rather expected to get a commendation for making a quick arrest, and maybe be a hero, but instead all I got was a good chuckle. However, the incident became one of the little secrets in my confidential file; a secret to be guarded. In similar experiences over the years, I have protected confidences to eliminate trouble for the persons involved, and thereby have accumulated a fund of information which has been invaluable in sizing up and solving other incidents.

Law enforcement, by nature, is monotonous, often grim and sometimes dangerous, but occasionally something amusing happens to lighten the policeman's burden. Along my way from rookie patrolman to Chief, I can remember other episodes which I can chuckle over now, although some of them were not altogether funny at the time.

Such was the story of Mr. X, a prominent business man of Beverly Hills. Shortly after the repeal of Prohibition, he was seated at a table in a Hollywood bar enjoying his new freedom to drink as he pleased. Furthermore, he was making a night of it, out on the town and in the mood for romantic adventure. His wife, of course, thought he was working late at the office.

For some time now he had been noticing an attractive woman sitting alone at another table. He had leveled numerous appraising glances toward her, and felt that she was not unaware of his interest. She looked well-dressed, refined and lonesome, but obviously too much of a lady to be easily approached. However, there would be no harm in sending her a polite note by the waiter, suggesting that she allow him to join her and buy her a drink.

With some little ceremony he dispatched the note, which came back shortly with a prim reply that she was not the type to let a stranger pick her up. However, she would make an exception in his case, since he looked like a respectable business man whom a lady could trust.

Mr. X was delighted. He moved to her table, ordered drinks, and began to enjoy a charming evening with his new-found friend. As the hour grew late the woman announced that she really must go home. When Mr. X offered to take her, she refused, saying the distance was too far. At first she would not tell him where she lived, but after much persuasion she revealed her home was in Beverly Hills. Well, that was exactly where Mr. X was going anyhow, and there was no good reason why she should not ride with him. After some more lady-like hesitancy she accepted his offer, and a short time later they parked in front of a handsome apartment house in our city.

The lady tried to say good-night outside the apartment, but Mr. X would not hear of it. He insisted they have a night-cap and, after considerable fencing she invited him in for a drink, and he accompanied her upstairs into a nicely furnished apartment. After another drink, he proposed that he stay for the rest of the night, and could hardly believe his luck when the lady agreed. He removed his coat and pants in the bed-room and, at her suggestion, went to the bathroom for a shower. He didn't hear the lock on the door click while he was showering. When he attempted to rejoin his charming companion he found himself locked in. He kicked and pounded on the door, and shouted, and finally broke the door open to make a sad discovery. The refined lady had disappeared, along with his coat, pants, wallet, keys and automobile.

The first thing the police department knew about Mr. X's predicament was when the switchboard at the station lit up like a three-alarm fire, with calls from various citizens report-

41

ing a nearly nude man in the street. It was a chilly morning, too. I was in charge of the morning watch, from midnight to 8 A.M., and when the desk officer reported the calls to me I went with the police car to the scene of the excitement. We found our man shivering in his BVDs outside the apartment house, looking for his automobile.

After hearing his story we examined the apartment and found that the woman had nothing in it. This was during the depression when apartment houses were having a hard time finding tenants. Landlords would rent an apartment for a small down payment and hope for the rest later. In this case Mr. X's girl friend had made a $10 deposit earlier in the day to get the apartment, then had skipped out after locking him in.

We hauled him to the station in the police car. His teeth were chattering from the cold when we arrived, so we furnished him with a blanket from the jail. He was an important citizen, but he looked awfully crestfallen as he sat in the office, wrapped in the blanket, repeating over and over, "How am I going to explain this to my wife? You've got to help me!" We were sympathetic but advised him that this was not the responsibility of the police department.

Finally, after much pleading on his part, I agreed to take him home, since he lived only a short distance from the station. At daybreak, I bundled him into a police car, still in the blanket, and delivered him to the front porch of his home. I had to take the blanket back with me, of course, so I unwrapped him as he rang the doorbell, and left him standing in his BVDs.

When his wife, red-eyed and sleepless, opened the door, Mr. X exclaimed: "Honey, I've been robbed! Isn't that right, officer?" turning to me. I had to agree that it was. "And they took my pants and coat and car keys so I couldn't report it. Isn't that right, officer?" Like a good straight man, I again nodded agreement.

Two days later his keys and wallet, minus the money, were returned to him in the mail, and his car was recovered later. He was the victim of a type of operation that was not uncommon in the Los Angeles metropolitan area during the depression. However, we have had no other trouble with Mr. X since that chilly morning.

Probably my funniest arrest was the time I chased down a drunk-driving woman on Wilshire Boulevard when I was a walking patrolman. Her car came weaving down the street toward me, while other motorists dodged to avoid it. Some cars did not dodge fast enough and were sideswiped. I commandeered one of the damaged cars, stood on the running-board, and ordered the driver to pursue the woman's car. We overtook the zigzagging vehicle after a six-block chase. When it slowed down I jumped to the running-board, reached in, and pulled on the brake.

I moved the woman out of the driver's seat and took the wheel myself, to drive her to the station. Unfortunately, the car, a huge and expensive Auburn, had a new-fangled gearshift on the dashboard which I had never encountered before. I got it started in the right direction, but try as I would I could not get it out of low gear. We proceeded slowly along Wilshire and turned up Rexford Drive toward the station, and as I kept on struggling with the gearshift lever my prisoner observed, scornfully: "You're drunker than I am!"

At the station, when I requested her to get out of the car, she was so intoxicated she began to put up a battle. She was a tiny woman who probably did not weigh more than 105 pounds, but she did not want to be arrested. With the help of another officer I removed her from the car and we carried her bodily to the booking desk. She slugged and kicked all the way, but luckily she was such a lightweight I didn't notice the blows. In other arrests, I've had to deal with husky, buxom women who swung and kicked so hard I'd feel the effects for several days afterwards.

Night patrol duty was often interesting. On one occasion I was driving a patrol car on Lexington Road at 3 A.M., at a location where a row of tall pine trees made the street darker than Wuthering Heights at midnight. I noticed a parked car with three men in it, all apparently asleep, and I circled back,

43

with headlights off, to investigate. Quietly pulling up behind the suspicious car, I got out and approached on foot. As I looked in I saw a gun on one of the men. I quickly swung the car door open, covered them with flashlight and gun, and ordered them to come out with their hands up. They came out fast, yelling, "Hey! Don't shoot! We're guards!"

They were private detectives who had been hired to guard a prominent person visiting a resident of our city. To ward off the chill of a cold California morning they had consumed a bottle of whiskey in the car and dozed off. After identifying themselves, they were greatly embarrassed and asked me to say nothing about the incident. Their client was paying them a good fee to guard him, and he might be unhappy to hear they had been asleep on the job.

On another night I was walking patrol in a dark alley behind a building which had recently been burglarized, when suddenly I stepped directly on top of a sleeping man. He let out a yell which echoed to the hills, and I went straight up in the air. He was not a drunk, I discovered, but a hard-up itinerant who had chosen the alley as a peaceful place to sleep.

Police work has interested me ever since my childhood in Providence, Rhode Island. My father was a patrolman in the old Third Precinct, and frequently drove the magnificent team of horses which pulled the patrol wagon. The Third Precinct included a rough area along the waterfront, frequented by brawny longshoremen and laborers. In those days, without our modern mechanical aids, men developed huge muscles shoveling coal from barges, lifting beer kegs, and doing other heavy manual labor. On Saturday nights, we would occasionally witness some bloody fistfights.

I grew up admiring the police for their courage and physical stamina in handling these tough customers. Policemen worked 12 hours a day then, and it was a hard life, but they were proud of the fact that they were upholding law and order. I figured it was a good career for red-blooded young men.

After finishing high school and a college business course,

44

I joined the Coast Guard and was stationed along the Maine coast. One winter there was enough to make me think of California. I remember freezing my wrists just above the glove line, and my ankles above the shoetops, and the tips of my ears were always subject to frostbite. One day at a lifesaving station, with the thermometer at 10 below, I picked up a magazine with a story about sunny Southern California. I regarded this as a personal message, calling me to the land of sunshine.

I wanted to be a policeman, because I liked action, adventure and an outdoor life. My first stop was Pasadena, where there was no police job open, but they did need a fireman. I didn't like this work, particularly, but I stayed with it for four years, and used my free time to study criminal law. When an opportunity arose to take the Beverly Hills Police Department examination, I was ready and waiting.

I changed jobs rapidly. At 8 A.M. one day I quit working as a Pasadena fireman, and at four o'clock in the afternoon started as a Beverly Hills patrolman. As time went on I became a detective, detective sergeant, lieutenant, captain, and assistant chief. In 1942, I became Chief.

Police work has never been boring for me. I still have my suits altered to allow for sidearms, ride patrol cars occasionally, and am on call 24 hours a day. In the event of any major crime, I am notified immediately.

Since Beverly Hills is one of the most glamorous high-income areas in the United States, our work here requires finesse more than strong-arm tactics. We have no slums, or factory districts or tenements, which breed crime in larger cities, but we do have 24-karat wealth which attracts criminals from far and near. To keep these gentry under surveillance, our detective roving squad visits fashionable cocktail bars and cafes, looking for confidence men in expensive silk suits, high-class "hookers" in mink coats, gigolos with wealthy widows, and other interesting criminal types.

We watch bars and night spots closely. An experienced detective can go into a place and almost immediately pick out the people who are up to no good. Unchaperoned women and lone men are generally suspect if they approach others at a bar. We are one of the few cities that have an ordinance requiring fingerprints of employees in places where liquor is served. It is helpful to officers to know the backgrounds of bartenders and waitresses. We don't hold their past against them, if they've been in trouble with the law, but if they get out of line our file on them is useful.

Beverly Hills detectives are sometimes "social lions." Because of the large number of wealthy and prominent citizens whose activities attract attention, we frequently assign detectives to guard large parties and receptions and keep an eye on the action. I am happy to say that these members of our force, well-dressed men in tuxedos, are an asset to every event they attend.

I am invited to many social functions. I like to think it's because I'm popular, but somehow I have a feeling that I'm really in demand more for protection. Even if I don't go in person, the police department is represented at any gathering where the assembled wealth might be an overpowering temptation to criminals, or where traffic direction and crowd-handling are needed. The star-spangled opening of the new Beverly Hilton Hotel, for example, required the services of 50 policemen.

When the late Evalyn Walsh McLean of Washington, D.C., leased a large Spanish-style home in Benedict Canyon, and brought the Hope diamond here, I was concerned by newspaper announcements of her plans for a large party at which, it was reported, she would wear the million-dollar bauble. Since she was a newcomer in our midst, I went to the house and interviewed her regarding her guest list, to make sure she had not been taken in by any unreliable characters. I suggested that the police department would rest easier if she would not wear the Hope diamond at such a public gathering. "What's the use of having it, if I can't wear it?," she asked. I didn't have a good answer for that one.

The party went on as planned. It was a glittering success,

overflowing with celebrities, furs and jewels. The Hope diamond, sparkling on its owner's neck, was the center of attention all evening. But it was never out of sight of a detective.

I was once one of 50 policemen and detectives assigned to guard the house and grounds of a wealthy industrialist during the wedding of his daughter. At the reception, I was admiring a collection of paintings and antiques in the library, where I was stationed, when the owner entered with last-minute instructions. "Please keep your eye on those books," he said, pointing to a high bookcase filled with matching leather-bound volumes, "They cost me a thousand dollars apiece!" I looked closer at the books and saw that each one had been individually hand-painted along the edges. Nobody touched the books while I was there.

We frequently guard the homes of families in Beverly Hills when important weddings or funerals are scheduled. Crooks read newspapers, too, and find tempting targets in mansions left unguarded while the families are away attending these functions.

At large hotel parties, we watch to see that departing guests don't try to claim the wrong fur coats, and at dinner dances in public places we usually have someone around to discourage the old dodge of switching fur coats which have been left on chairs while their owners are dancing. We have a real sneaky trap for "car clouters," who steal valuables from parked automobiles. We leave an expensive-looking fur coat in a parked sedan, and station detectives to watch the bait at a discreet distance.

Police here are alerted to track down annoyers of prominent women. Many Beverly Hills women are active in society, and their pictures in newspapers frequently make them targets for telephone calls from unbalanced men who attempt to flirt, or threaten them, or become obscene. Telephone annoyers are a problem everywhere, and more so in a city with well-publicized society women.

We have never had a riot in rich, law-abiding Beverly Hills. Instead of civil disorder we have traffic-stopping events, such as the Howard Hughes plane crash, the first Elizabeth Taylor wedding, and motion-picture openings which we call "gala premieres." All such tie up traffic, and traffic is our problem. We are in a metropolitan area of 6,000,000 population, located across the main east-west boulevards which link Los Angeles to the Pacific Ocean. Consequently, a flood of 400,000 automobiles flows through our exclusive little city every day.

Traffic officers still talk about the big tie-up of 1946 when Howard Hughes, the millionaire aviator-industrialist, crashed his large experimental plane, the XF-11, at the edge of Beverly Hills on a Sunday afternoon in July, when thousands of motorists were on their way home from the beaches. Mr. Hughes was attempting to land the crippled plane on the grounds of the Los Angeles Country Club, but it fell short. Several persons missed death by a whisper as the big plane sheared its 101-foot wing through two residences on North Linden Drive and burst into flames as it hit a third home on North Whittier Drive.

The first citizen to call the fire department was Actor Dennis O'Keefe, who saw it all from his home across the street. Luckily, a young Marine sergeant, William Lloyd Durkin, was on hand to pull Mr. Hughes from the wreckage. Firemen battled the blaze for three hours. Next day a patrolman found Mr. Hughes's good-luck charm, an old felt hat, in the bottom of the cockpit. The crash sent a pyre of smoke hundreds of feet in the air, visible for miles, and drew thousands of sightseers to the area. Police worked for hours afterward getting the streets unjammed.

Although less spectacular than the Hughes crash, the wedding of Elizabeth Taylor, screen star, and Conrad Hilton, Jr., was a crowd-puller. People covered the lawn and sidewalks around the Church of the Good Shepherd, and stood four-deep across the street, waiting to see the bride and groom and the movie stars among the 700 invited guests. A score of policemen, including security guards from the M-G-M Studios, were required to handle the crowd and keep traffic moving along

Santa Monica Boulevard. It was a hometown event. The 18-year-old bride not only was called "the most beautiful girl in the world," but also had lived here ever since her parents brought her from England as a child. Her father had an art gallery in the Beverly Hills Hotel for a number of years. The groom was the handsome 23-year-old son of America's most famous hotel millionaire, socially prominent here and in the East. It was our big romantic moment of the year 1950.

Important film openings, which bring out spotlights, movie stars, limousines, microphones, television cameras, photographers, reporters, columnists, correspondents, and crowds of cheering spectators, often keep 50 or more policemen busy for several hours. We have a dozen or so of these every year, and since many of our residents are prominent in "The Industry," we enjoy close working relationships with the police departments of the surrounding major motion-picture studios.

Labor unions and strikes are not a problem in Beverly Hills, although the city has been in on the fringe of minor labor disturbances. Occasionally pickets from a strike-bound factory or store in the Greater Los Angeles area come all the way to Beverly Hills to picket the home of the boss, or of an executive of the company involved. On a different sector of the labor front, officers of the Allied Industrial Workers were forced to close the union's swank international headquarters on Wilshire Boulevard in 1958, and move the head office to Milwaukee to be nearer the membership. Eastern members of the union had protested against the luxury of having their headquarters in Beverly Hills! Union officers agreed to the move reluctantly, pointing out that the land they had bought here in 1954 for $600 to $700 a front-foot was worth twice as much in 1958.

five

NO PARADISE

FOR POLICEMEN

BEVERLY HILLS IS SAID TO HAVE MORE LAWYERS PER capita than any other city in the world—one attorney to every 40 residents, roughly. This abundance of hometown legal talent in a well-to-do community affects the work of the police in a curious way. With 750 lawyers on hand, and with most of our citizens financially able to hire expert legal counsel, minor arrests here frequently become court cases. Even a speeding ticket may develop into a lawsuit.

Usually, when John Q. Public is picked up for speeding, he will pay his fine and go home, resolved to drive more carefully in the future. In Beverly Hills, however, the defendant is likely to show up in court with two lawyers, plead "not guilty," and spend $1000 in legal fees in an attempt to avoid a small fine.

Wealth makes for opinionated people, and we have some very wealthy ones. Some of them have been known to fight traffic tickets merely because the arresting officer failed to recognize them!

Beverly Hills police, therefore, have to make sure of their facts and their legal status in every arrest, and file accurate reports in even the most minor cases.

I remember one fast-driving business man we picked up for speeding. Residents along Sunset Boulevard had complained that every morning, at almost exactly the same time, a speeding sports car roared around a curve on this scenic drive. On Saturday and Sunday mornings, however, all was quiet, indicating that the driver was somebody who was going to his office five days a week.

We stationed a motorcycle officer to watch the curve. He did not have long to wait. At the appointed hour a red sports car whizzed past him, and the officer gave chase successfully. The driver, a jaunty, middle-aged citizen, was a nationally-known executive, and he was aggressively unhappy about getting a speeding ticket.

When the report reached my desk I sensed trouble ahead and alerted the traffic officers to go back to the scene and measure the distance the motorcycle had chased the car, to establish the time elapsed after the officer saw the car until he caught it, and to check with the Harley-Davidson company as to how fast one of their motorcycles could travel in that time, from a standing start. "This man has an office full of engineers working for him," I told the officers. "He will likely come into court with technical men and drawings to fight the charge, and we will have to be ready for him."

As I predicted, the speeder confidently arrived in court flanked by engineers, and with a most imposing diagram five feet long on which had been sketched not only a portion of Sunset Boulevard but the trees and shrubbery as well. He put up a good fight, but we were prepared with our equally technical testimony. He pleaded "not guilty" and lost.

Since there are more important people living here than in other cities of our size, we sometimes have trouble with influential citizens who try to bring pressure on the police department to protect themselves. On one occasion we had to arrest a prominent member of a local church on a drunk charge. He

51

alibied to his wife, and complained vehemently that we were wrong. His wife, in turn, protested to the Mayor so vigorously that he was almost persuaded we had made a mistake. However, such cases usually solve themselves. A short time later our man was picked up in Hollywood by the Los Angeles police for drunk driving.

The years have taught me that almost everybody in trouble wants to blame somebody else for his predicament. Thus both the drunk driver and the man caught stealing may try to put the blame on the policeman who arrests them. I have seen drunks brought into the station carrying an alcoholic content high enough to blow our Breathalyzer out of commission, who will indignantly deny it later and accuse the arresting officer of error.

In general, Beverly Hills is one of the most law-abiding communities in the United States. Except for traffic arrests, fewer than two per cent of the arrests made here are residents of the city. Our criminals come from the outside. Few Beverly Hills property owners have been involved in violent crimes, and it was a great shock to the community some years ago when a man who had been considered a respectable citizen was caught robbing a bank in another city.

In 30 years, we have had only seven or eight murders, except for murder-suicides, and only two which got national attention: the gang-style slaying of mobster Bugsy Siegel, and the killing of Johnny Stompanato by Lana Turner's daughter.

Most of our few murders have been among domestics employed here. In one case a maid stabbed her mistress to death in an argument over the proper method of boning meat. In another instance, a Beverly Hills housewife reported a murder by telephoning her husband in Chicago, instead of the local police. In this case, two Filipino housemen, who were physical culture fans, lived and kept their bar-bells in the basement of the apartment house where they worked. One houseman won a considerable sum of money in a Chinese lottery in a neighboring city and took it home with him. His envious roommate slugged him to death with a bar-bell, and carried the body in a laundry sack to an automobile.

The housewife, looking out her window, saw the man hauling away his curious load, and voiced her suspicions by telephone to her husband in Chicago. He told her she was imagining things and to forget it. Next day, however, her curiosity triumphed and she asked the manager of the apartment house where his housemen were. When he could not locate them he called police. We found blood on the floor of their room and suspected foul play. Later a Japanese gardener found the body of the houseman in a field near Culver City which had been flooded by a recent rainstorm. The murderer had dumped it there, thinking it was an ocean inlet, but the water subsided and revealed the body. We traced the killer to Alaska and the Philippine Islands, but he got away, and disappeared during the Japanese occupation of the islands.

Beverly Hills policemen sometimes get into dilemmas as defenders of the morals of the community. We had one conscientious patrolman who was approached by two women with complaints that an art dealer was displaying indecent statuary in his show-window. The officer promptly investigated and found several statuettes in the window which were replicas of famous Michelangelo sculptures. The officer had never been to Rome or Florence and didn't know that the originals have been on display for centuries, but he could see that the figures were nude and unmistakably male. Doing his duty as he saw it, he told the art dealer he would have to remove the statuettes from the window. The dealer called the newspapers, who had a field day at our expense. Art critics sent caustic letters suggesting that to avoid future incidents I should start a class in art history and appreciation.

Another patrolman protected the tender sensibilities of his district by censoring a sign on a Wilshire Boulevard movie theater. The manager was proudly admiring his new marquee billing, which blazoned out the words "A Helluva Show!," when the patrolman approached with a suggestion. As the patrolman walked away the sign read: "A Heck of a Show!"

We had some unexpected visitors in 1957 when a Las Vegas resort set up a demonstration gambling layout on Wilshire Boulevard and invited the public in to learn the fundamentals of games of chance, as a publicity stunt. The Nevada boys had everything a gambler could want, dice table, roulette wheel, blackjack table and birdcage, and served free coffee, sandwiches and potato chips. I pointed out that possession of gambling equipment is a violation of California law, and closed up the operation an hour and a half after it opened. Somehow, it didn't seem right to be teaching Beverly Hills people to gamble so they could lose their money in Las Vegas.

Our well-heeled community is frequently the target of hold-up men who view it as a sort of promised land. Fortunately, we have been able to cope with them successfully. Recently an unemployed young husband in San Fernando Valley went berserk after a quarrel with his wife, and headed for Beverly Hills "to find some rich person to rob." He dressed formally for the occasion, in dinner jacket and black tie, and rode to one of our prominent hotels in a cab. On the fourth floor of the hotel he invaded a room where a gay reunion party was in progress, and terrorized the party into submission by firing at the ceiling. He announced he was there to "rob the rich," and fired a shot through the door at a hotel detective who arrived to investigate the noise. When I arrived at the scene, after a summons from the hotel, police officers had the room surrounded, but the gunman refused to come out. He fired another shot at us through the door, and we threatened to throw tear gas in the room unless he surrendered. He finally came out, and when the door opened we were surprised to see nine people in the room. They were delighted to see us.

The screwiest stick-up man I ever encountered was Jack Dugdale, an ex-convict from Canada, who walked into a Beverly Hills house in broad daylight and robbed the occupants at gunpoint. On his hasty getaway, Dugdale ran into a type of situation that has always intrigued me as a police offi-

54

cer. It seems that he was almost in the clear when he made the mistake of driving his getaway car through a boulevard stop. One of our patrol cars was quietly pursuing its rounds and gave chase, quickly overtaking the car. The officer was writing out a simple traffic ticket when his partner in the patrol car received the radio report of the robbery identifying Dugdale and the charge thereupon went from misdemeanor to felony. This is a good example of many I have seen when routine, often monotonous law enforcement, through alertness on the part of conscientious officers often trips up very dangerous criminals. After serving a term in State prison, he returned to our city and pulled exactly the same type of mid-day hold-up, and again was caught within five minutes. This time he went to prison for life as an habitual criminal.

I had a close call with him in the station. He repeatedly begged us to take off his handcuffs, and wrung his hands in a great display of distress. Puzzled by his actions, I felt around his shirt and found another loaded gun in his waistband. If we had listened to his plea and taken off the handcuffs he would have started shooting.

Recently I noticed the influence of television "westerns" on gunmen. We arrested a gang of three men who had robbed three restaurants, after tracing them to their rooms in West Hollywood, where we found a full-length mirror filled with bullet holes. They had been using it to practice quick draws.

The last time I shot a man in line of duty was some years ago when I arrested a suspect at a gasoline filling station in West Los Angeles. He admitted his identity, and stood still for questioning, but when I leaned over to frisk him for weapons he slugged me hard on the jaw, jolting me, and started running. I ran after him and called on him to stop, but he put on more speed and went up and over a high wire fence surrounding the old Harold Lloyd movie lot, where the Mormon Temple is today. I shot at him and creased his side just as he cleared the fence, but he dropped on the other side and got away. Weeks later I got a call from the County Morgue. They had the body of a man who had been killed in an attempted robbery, who resembled my fugitive. I went to the morgue and found my man, with the bullet scar in his side.

Physical danger and hardship, however, are not the most hazardous aspects of a policeman's life. Far more bothersome are the unanticipated and unjustifiable law suits brought against him as harassment. Anyone who has the price of a lawyer's fee can sue, and the police department is a popular target because of the nature of its duties. Many such suits are instituted only to aid a defendant in a police case by beclouding the issue. Other suits are brought by lawyers representing left-wing groups whose aim is to harass the police and discredit law enforcement. Suits are frequently launched by publicity seekers, politically ambitious individuals, or other persons with hidden motives.

I have been sued for more than $1,000,000 damages for actions I have taken in performance of my duty as a policeman over the years, and this in a small, law-abiding city. The grand total of damage suits filed against law officers in other American cities is a staggering figure. Obviously, I could not afford to be a policeman, at these prices, were it not for the fact that in all the suits filed against me to date only one judgment was granted against me, and it was later reversed. This is indicative of the questionable status of such suits. As Chief of Police, I am co-defendant in most of the civil suits filed against members of the department also.

The campaign of harassment which left-wing and ill-advised groups have waged against police departments everywhere has paid off in a way that must make the Communist Party happy. The average American today, in my opinion, has less respect for law enforcement than his grandfather had.

Legal technicalities which delay justice have also lowered the average man's opinion of law enforcement. Citizens tend to get disillusioned about justice when a known criminal with an expensive staff of lawyers can fight off sentencing for years on a technicality, or escape scotfree through a legal loophole.

Moral standards have been relaxed and the public conscience lulled. In earlier days a man convicted of a felony was not so quickly forgiven by his fellow-citizens. They withheld judgment until his conduct demonstrated that his sentence had had a salutary effect. Today, if a felon has money enough, he is socially acceptable almost anywhere.

We have had Communists and fellow-travelers in Beverly Hills, among them some "Hollywood Reds," but the police department has been aware of their activity ever since the late 1930s. We know the difference between a legitimate book-review club and a Communistic "study group," and we were not unaware of Paul Robeson's visit to our city some years ago. Through the years we have kept the Federal Bureau of Investigation advised of Communistic activities here. There have even been Beverly Hills lawyers cited by the Un-American Activities Committee.

A substantial majority of the men in the legal profession are of high ideals and character, but in my years of service I have also encountered some who were unethical, unscrupulous, and even lawbreakers. I have known some who tried to intimidate officers, or even bribe them. No profession is free from moral weaklings, but too often it is the policeman who is held up as a horrible example of human frailty in character. It should be remembered that when a police officer accepts a bribe it is usually because someone else has suggested it to him. In the few cases I've had of policemen who failed to carry out their duties according to the rules and regulations of the department, lawyers have contributed to a majority of these transgressions.

There have been attorneys who raised false charges of police brutality in an attempt to confuse jurors and gain sympathy for their clients. I remember one case of a drunk we rescued from a burning apartment house. He didn't want to be saved, and put up such a battle officers had to remove him by force. In the struggle he got bruised, and a complaint was filed with the County Grand Jury, alleging police brutality. When the hearing was called, the drunk did not show up. He was in San Francisco. But we insisted on appearing and told

57

our story to the Grand Jury and were vindicated. Considering the thousands arrested every year, there have been remarkably few incidents of personal conflict between the people and the police. The percentage is less than one-half of 1 per cent here, out of an annual total of 3000 arrests for all types of criminal offenses.

During the depression of the 1930s we arrested a whole gang of rubbish collectors, all White Russians from Boyle Heights in Los Angeles, who had a tire-stealing operation going. Their technique was simple and noisy. While one member of the gang made a tremendous amount of racket loading rubbish into a truck, his pals would break into nearby gas stations and steal tires, hauling them away with the rubbish and selling them. When we caught the men they were originally charged with grand theft. However, since the minimum for grand theft is $200, the charge was later reduced to petty theft, and the attorney for one of the defendants was allowed to plead him guilty to several counts of petty theft. Afterwards the attorney charged his client $500 extra, telling him the money was for the judge and the police as a "pay off" for reducing the charge. Actually, his client was entitled to the lesser charge, and the lawyer's lie only served to defame honest law officers. We learned about it later when the client complained.

Another lawyer charged a defendant an exorbitant fee for pleading him guilty to drunk-driving, leading him to believe that he had been in a more serious fix from which the lawyer had rescued him by his clever pleading. However, the only charge against the man had been simple drunk driving.

In recent years, because of liberal verdicts awarded by juries in personal injury suits, traffic accidents have become a financial racket. I have noticed a striking increase in the number of personal injury claims arising from automobile collisions in Beverly Hills. In earlier years here, we used to take traffic crashes as a matter of course where there were no obvious injuries, and officers did not hesitate to report their opinion on the extent of injuries, if any. Lawyers are aware of the situation today. When one of Bing Crosby's sons was involved in a very minor traffic accident recently, lawyers investigating it arrived at the police station almost as soon as the traffic officer's report!

Every police officer sooner or later finds himself the target of a campaign. My turn came as the result of an arrest of two women for prostitution. The girls were highly surprised by the arrest because they had been paying two local lawyers $50 a month each for what they had been told was "protection." We picked up the two attorneys, who admitted receiving the money but insisted it was only a retainer fee. I was in favor of locking them up in jail, but I was a lieutenant at the time and was overruled. All we had was the word of the prostitutes against the lawyers, but I was convinced the girls were telling the truth, and that the attorneys had misrepresented their status in order to collect the payments.

I soon found myself the target of these attorneys, who had connections with some unethical bail bondsmen. Shortly after I became Chief of Police, in order to safeguard the interests of persons arrested and confined in City Jail, we adopted strict rules regulating the activities of bail bondsmen and unethical attorneys in the jail. These new regulations resulted in a financial loss to both the bail bondsmen and unscrupulous attorneys. This group then secretly banded together in an attempt to oust me and replace me with a more liberal subordinate, but a strong City Council and the leading business men stood by me, and we made our policy stick.

I have often been threatened with retaliation for taking a stand on certain issues, but I have found that if I am on the side of law and order I have nothing to fear. I do not dabble in politics, but stay with law enforcement and its problems. To be effective, a policeman must be devoted to law enforcement and believe in it enthusiastically, convinced that right will prevail. He must disregard unfair criticism, false accusations, and the ever-present harassment of law suits.

six

WOLVES

AND WOMEN

BECAUSE BEVERLY HILLS HAS MORE THAN ITS SHARE OF wealth, lonesome divorcees and susceptible rich widows, it attracts "wolves," gigolos, confidence men and fortune-hunters in unusually large numbers. All these predators are interested in money, rather than love, but too often their female victims have foolishly let themselves be swindled, winding up broken-hearted as well as broke.

Fortunately, our police department knows how to spot rogue males, has a list of the most successful ones, and is familiar with their *modus operandi*. I doubt if policemen in any other city have had as much experience in this kind of work.

"Con men" of this type dress immaculately, drive sporty cars, and reek of sophistication. If they have jobs, their employment does not require much of their time. They are most attentive to women, with flowers, birthday presents and compliments, sprinkling a few pennies around to get dollar bills.

They have many opportunities here, because wealthy women, socially inclined, don't like to be seen alone at restaurants, theaters, parties, movie premieres and similar social events. Sometimes the women take up with escorts as a temporary convenience, and later find the escorts don't want to be dropped. The con men get in by courtesy and attentiveness until they have their prey hooked, then hold them by fear of bodily harm or adverse publicity.

Unfortunately, police protection is usually resented by the women involved. Some adults are too old to spank and too immature to realize the danger of certain associations. Many times we have had to look on helplessly as a gigolo fastened on to the fortune of a foolish woman, waiting for an overt act that would justify police action, and often our help comes too late.

Personal warnings seldom do any good; the victim is so charmed by her companion that she takes offense at outsiders who offer advice. Often I've warned prospective victims, only to have them relay my report to the con men, who then assumed an air of righteous indignation and descended on City Hall threatening law suits—but never filing them.

I remember particularly well a banker's widow who had led a discreet and sheltered life while her husband was alive. After his death left her an estate of several million dollars, she moved to glamorous Beverly Hills and started on a fling. She bought a mansion with a walk-in marble bath and marble staircase, and began entertaining. Personal appearance became an obsession with her. She visited a beauty shop three or four times a week, and went through an unusual beauty ritual at home which required a daily bath in gallons of coffee cream, followed by a lengthy massage.

The widow could not be disturbed while in the cream bath. The first time I was called to the house on a police investigation, I sat in the reception hall cooling my heels until the ritual was over. On later calls, I arranged to arrive after Madam had finished her beauty treatments.

She lived in Asiatic splendor, her pleasure palace filled with servants. She enjoyed being seen at night spots with handsome young men, and there were always young men available.

Inevitably, she got involved with a series of gigolos who, in turn, took her for considerable sums of money. Her husband had left everything in trust to safeguard her, but the gigolos encouraged her to find lawyers who would break the trust, and finally even got rid of the trust officer.

She met one of these con men at a Hollywood party, a charming fellow to whom she confided that she was lonesome and, despite her wealth, unhappy. She had many friends, she said, but no dear friends. She complimented him on his dancing, and offered him $300 a month to be her companion and escort to dances. He took the job, naturally, and later $40,000 in "gifts."

After much of her money was gone, she moved into a $400-a-month apartment and took up with another young male escort, who ransacked her apartment while she was relaxing in Palm Springs. Among other things, she missed a 5-carat diamond ring. She complained to the police, but after we established the fact that he had stolen from her she refused to prosecute. All she wanted was to hold the threat of prosecution over his head so that he would stay with her.

She was an unhappy victim of her ego, refusing to admit defeat, even though her boy friend, who was thriving on her money, had set up housekeeping in another apartment with a gorgeous young redhead. In a few years she dissipated the entire fortune, and when she died left an estate of less than $10,000.

I remember another occasion, however, when I was able to stop a fortune-hunter cold, and save a wealthy girl from unhappiness. She was a visitor from the East who had flown to Beverly Hills for a vacation. She stopped at one of our best hotels, but found her room was not yet ready. A local Beau Brummel overheard the room clerk apologizing for the delay, and gallantly offered his assistance. He suggested a lunch while she waited for the room, and since he looked like a gentleman she accepted his invitation.

Beau Brummel put on quite a show at lunch. He dropped some references to a silver fox farm he owned near Reno, and made a fine impression as a substantial business man. As their friendship grew, nourished by a dinner date that evening, he learned that the girl was from a wealthy family and had considerable money of her own. Inspired by this knowledge he redoubled his campaign, escorting her to the racetrack, restaurants and dances, with fresh flowers for every occasion. Within 48 hours he proposed marriage and the fascinated young woman accepted. Love was wonderful, she thought, and so sudden—just like in the movies!

Eager to share her happiness, she called her brother in Washington, D.C., to give him the news. When the brother, an attorney, found out how little his sister knew of the background of her fiance, he prudently and immediately telephoned the manager of the hotel in Beverly Hills, asking for information on the man. The manager knew nothing about him, but said he would call the Chief of Police.

I was able to tell him quite a bit. The man was an ex-convict whom we had picked up twice before when he had taken women for money. I suggested to the manager that we have lunch together next day at a table near the "lovebirds." As I entered the hotel dining-room the following noon I noticed the fortune-hunter and his intended victim at their table, and moved in their direction. When he saw me the man quickly hid his face behind the 14-inch menu card, and pretended to study it closely as he ordered lunch. Nor did he look up when the manager and I sat down at the next table.

As I rose after a pleasant lunch I looked over and said cordially, "Hello, George. How's the wife and baby?" The man mustered a sickly smile, but said nothing. I could see that the girl was extremely annoyed, however. She looked daggers at her escort and at me, as I walked out with the manager. Minutes later she came out of the room alone, looking for the manager. She wanted to know who I was. When he told her I was the Chief of Police, she came over to me and asked me what I knew about the Beau Brummel. I don't remember whether or not she thanked me, but she made airplane reservations immediately afterward and flew home the same day.

Just to make sure that the man would bother her no more, I had officers pick him up and warn him to leave her alone.

Beau's next victim was less fortunate. After getting a divorce from the wife who had handicapped his game, he went on a social prowl in the East and met a wealthy widow from a prominent Kentucky family. Their "romance" started at a Derby Day party in Louisville. (Con men are always on hand for the top social and sporting events, whether in New York, Miami, or elsewhere.) She was an attractive 40-year-old brunette who had recently lost her husband and was vulnerable. He posed as a well-to-do business man with a home in Beverly Hills, and swept her off her feet with a skillful courtship.

Not long after their marriage Beau persuaded his wife to sell her old Kentucky home and buy a new one near Beverly Hills. He stayed in California while she went East to arrange for the shipment of her personal property here, including expensive furniture and several cases of choice liquors. As his wife's goods arrived, Beau stored them in the garage, but when she returned she found the cases of liquor and other items missing. She discovered her new husband had sold them and pocketed the money.

Too late she learned the con man's true character. She wanted a divorce, but feared a scandal because of her prominence in Kentucky. Further, her husband said he would demand a handsome settlement. She came to me for advice, but since there is little police can do in a situation between husband and wife, I told her to see an attorney. She later decided to stay with the man, and they moved to another community, where she began drinking heavily to escape her embarrassment. The last word I heard was that she was a hopeless alcoholic. She was a victim of a tragic situation in which the police were powerless to help.

Both men and women are very vulnerable after an emotional experience, such as the loss of a husband or wife by death or divorce, and frequently will fall for anybody who is sympathetic to them.

An attractive man in Hot Springs, Arkansas, met a wealthy Beverly Hills widow there and followed her to California with a proposal of marriage which she accepted. He further charmed her by taking her to look at expensive homes in the most exclusive part of Beverly Hills, and even went through the motions of negotiating to buy a $125,000 residence. One morning he called her with a problem. He had to make a $2500 cash down payment on the house, and his money had not yet arrived from the East. Would she mind withdrawing the money from her account and giving it to him for the deal, temporarily? She was only too happy to help her sweetheart, and the money was delivered to him within the hour.

Her fiance then excused himself to go to the barber shop. He wanted to get freshened up for their trip to Las Vegas where they would be married the next day. He went to the barber shop and never came back, and neither did her money. We traced him and found he had pulled this trick on a number of women, including a schoolteacher in Denver, Colorado. Several States had placed "holds" on him. Later he was caught and jailed in Pennsylvania for a similar swindle. By this time however, the gullible Beverly Hills widow had remarried and had dropped charges against him.

And then there was the divorcee who met a handsome man in a local hotel. He claimed to be a famous major-league baseball pitcher, but he pitched romance instead. In a very short time he talked the lady into a trip to Las Vegas where, he told her, they would be married. Since his money was inconveniently tied up elsewhere (it always is!) he allowed his fiancee to pay his way to Nevada's Gretna Green, where she also paid for the marriage license and the wedding. After the wedding the bride soon discovered her new husband was an ex-convict instead of a baseball player. The police picked him up for passing bad checks while they were on their honeymoon.

We recently arrested a dapper 32-year-old man who had made an easy living for 13 years at fashionable resorts in Europe and America. When we questioned him we uncovered a case history typical of his kind. He had been a handsome and popular youth in high school near San Francisco, where he was president of his graduating class and named "the man most likely to succeed" in the yearbook. He succeeded, but in the wrong way. In college he majored in athletics instead of any serious study and quit school to become a "ski bum." In winter he worked as a ski instructor at winter resorts and in summer he taught water skiing at beach resorts. His favorite customers were lonesome women with money.

He traveled through Europe and America this way, meeting prominent people and living at top resorts, usually at someone else's expense. Always in the market for marriage, he wed one woman in France, another in Mexico and a third in the United States. As he moved on to each new romance he left a wife behind with the problem of getting an annulment or divorce.

He was arrested in Italy, Switzerland and Mexico after defrauding hotels, resorts and transportation companies out of thousands of dollars. He financed some of his trips with a stolen credit card, passed worthless checks, and once posed as a doctor to obtain credit. In Mexico he set a record of sorts by being arrested three times at exclusive resorts and escaping each time. In the United States he was involved with the law from Vermont to Florida as well as along the Pacific Coast, and spent more than two years in various city, county, State and Federal penal institutions.

We picked him up in Beverly Hills after he had made off with the automobile of a girl friend. When our officer stopped the car and began to question him, the ski expert suddenly put it in gear and drove away at high speed, dragging the officer with him. The officer fell from the car when it was traveling 70 miles an hour but miraculously was not killed. Meanwhile another police car pursued the suspect and fired a shot which brought him to a halt after a five mile chase.

When we brought the young man into headquarters he boasted of the number of women he had met, made love to, and taken for money during his gay life as an international crook. When he completes his present sentence I have no doubt

66

he will take up his "career" where he left off. Our study of the behavior of confidence artists shows that they seldom can give up their deceitful ways.

Another wealthy widow here met a man in a bar who posed as a successful business man and launched a whirlwind courtship. She was about to marry him when we interfered. His business was robbing banks—and he was not successful!

Police never underestimate the charm of a gigolo. We had a particularly frustrating experience some years ago when a local playboy ran away with several thousand dollars worth of jewelry belonging to a wealthy divorcee he had been "courting." We traced him to a Chicago-bound train and notified police in the Illinois city. They arrested him when he stepped off the train there. However, at this point the divorcee had a change of heart and tearfully refused to sign a complaint to extradite him. She was, she said, still in love with him!

Women are not the only victims of love swindlers. Wealthy men, even some smart fortune-hunters whose background is known to the police, have often been duped by unscrupulous females. One millionaire, who built up his wealth by a series of fortunate marriages, was victimized by a girl friend who tried to obtain money from him by a false accusation. She sued on behalf of her "unborn child" for a portion of his $300,000 annual income, charging that he was the father. She also claimed he had hired thugs to beat her up, causing her to lose the baby. A police investigation disproved her story, and, when no child was born after waiting a respectable number of months, the suit was ruled out of court.

A truck driver came to my office recently with a sad story. He had met a blonde through the Personal advertisements in a Los Angeles newspaper when he inserted an "object matrimony" ad. She lived in Beverly Hills and looked like a lovely prospect for marriage. He became infatuated with her, and spent money on her. But when he pressed her to set a wedding date, she turned on him. "I'm already married, you jerk," she had told him. "And what's more, my husband is a gangster who will beat you to a pulp if you are ever seen with me."

When he told me the name of the woman, I congratulated him on his good luck in getting off so easily. She was a known police character, who might have taken him for much more money.

Frequently our investigations of men who prey on wealthy women are hampered because of information which they have in their "little black books" concerning their victims. Usually it is of such a nature that the latter do not care to prosecute. I remember one case in which a wealthy widow was victimized by two gigolos, who knew she would not complain to the police, since she herself had acquired the money by marrying an old man under peculiar circumstances during a trip to Europe.

Yes, we seem to have more than our share of suave predatory males pursuing wealthy females in our star-studded city. Usually the major loss involves a rather common commodity in Beverly Hills: disillusionment. But all too frequently, from a poiceman's point of view, a great deal of money can be picked up by the sharp boys (and girls) who sell synthetic romance. No single case in my experience was as coldly tragic as that involving one of our most glamorous actresses, her fourteen-year-old daughter, and a punk mobster who was as attractive as he was vicious: Johnny Stompanato.

seven

LANA AND

JOHNNY

THE LAST TIME I SAW JOHNNY STOMPANATO HE WAS lying flat on his back in Lana Turner's bedroom, cold dead. He had been stabbed to death by Cheryl Crane, fourteen-year-old daughter of the blonde actress, at 9:40 P.M. on Good Friday, April 4, 1958.

Handsome Johnny was one of the most successful "wolves" in Hollywood. He was a man of mystery, whose activities had interested Los Angeles County law officers for several years. He had a police record, a newspaper reputation as a mobster's bodyguard, and he was catnip to the ladies.

Frequently seen in night clubs and cafes along the Sunset Strip, between Beverly Hills and Hollywood, Stompanato was popular as a dancing escort for movie stars and starlets. An ex-Marine, wavy-haired and muscular, he seemed to have a fascination for rich, beautiful and susceptible women. His matrimonial status was constantly changing, and confusing, to say the least.

We had considerable information on him. We knew he

had obtained large sums of money from individuals who were afraid to complain to the police, and we were aware that he had accepted money from a number of his women friends.

On one occasion, I had assisted him out the rear door of a prominent Beverly Hills hotel, holding him by the collar and the seat of his well tailored slacks, after he had become abusive during a police investigation. Had we known positively that he was there for the purpose of extorting money from a hotel guest, we could have saved his victim thousands of dollars, and Stompanato might have been alive today, and in prison.

Trained policemen can spot tragedy before it happens, and in Stompanato's case I had seen it coming for some time. Stompanato had fixed on Lana Turner after a divorce left her available. He called her at home, dropped a few names of people he knew, progressed to a cocktail party friendship with her. Soon the actress was in much deeper water than she had anticipated.

When information first reached the police department that Miss Turner was having trouble with her escort, I had predicted that such an association would inevitably end in tragedy. Several months before the killing we had had a report that Scotland Yard detectives had picked up Stompanato at a fashionable Chelsea apartment and hurried his departure from England after he had a violent quarrel with the actress there. Exactly one week before the slaying I received a telephone call from Mrs. Mabel Turner, mother of the actress, informing me that her daughter had become terribly frightened of this hoodlum. When she asked me what should be done, I advised her that her daughter should come in and report to the police immediately. This was never done.

I thought of these things that Good Friday night as I listened to Miss Turner's story of the killing. We were in a richly furnished upstairs room of her residence on North Bedford Drive, while a Fire Department resuscitator crew still worked over Stompanato's lifeless body in an adjacent bedroom.

Although her voice shook slightly, she appeared to be a remarkably composed woman under the circumstances. Stompanato, she said, had threatened to beat her up during a nasty quarrel. It was the climax of a series of battles which had begun earlier in London, where Johnny pursued her while she worked on a picture. When she had attempted to break off their relationship, Stompanato threatened to disfigure her with a razor and cripple her if she ever tried to leave him.

Tonight's quarrel had been the worst of all, she said. She was afraid of him because he had hurt her, was abusive and threatening, and her daughter, Cheryl, knew it. The girl had stood outside the door listening. When Miss Turner opened the door to order Stompanato out of the room, Cheryl rushed in and struck Stompanato.

"I didn't see any knife," said the actress. "I truthfully thought she had just poked him in the stomach. He didn't say a word, just gasped. He grabbed his stomach, walked a little way, half-turned and fell, dropping on his back. He didn't talk; he only kept gasping. He had his hands over his stomach. Finally they dropped away. I lifted his sweater and saw the blood. It's like a great nightmare. I can't believe it happened."

I then interrogated Cheryl, grave and frightened in her grandmother's care in another room. Cheryl's story was essentially the same as her mother's. "I didn't mean to kill him, I just meant to frighten him," she told me still shocked and unable to believe that Johnny Stompanato was dead.

It was a busy night for the police department. Regardless of my opinion of Stompanato, and knowledge of his past record, our investigation of his killing had to be made with an open mind, and conducted for the sole purpose of obtaining evidence on the person responsible and establishing the circumstances. Our investigation was intensified by the fact that Jerry Giesler, one of the outstanding criminal lawyers in the United States, had been brought into the case as the representative of Cheryl Crane. We were aware of his ability and his many years of experience in homicide cases, and we knew that if there were an error in our report it would be quickly detected. We established the facts of the killing beyond any question of a doubt.

Early Saturday morning, after Cheryl had been interrogated again at headquarters and lodged in the juvenile section of the City Jail, I returned home to rest, but not to sleep. My telephone rang like a cash register at a fire sale, with calls from newspapers all over the United States and Canada, and foreign correspondents. Each wanted the latest development in the case, but there were no more facts to give. After several hours of climbing in and out of bed, I gave up the idea of sleeping and went out for an early breakfast and to the office. Later in the day I returned to the scene of the killing with other officers to take measurements and prepare an exact diagram of the room, and again interrogated Miss Turner and others involved.

On Easter Sunday afternoon, while I was in my office reviewing the facts of our investigation, I received a visit from Carmine Stompanato, brother of the dead man, who arrived with two known police characters, Max Tannenbaum, of Brooklyn, and Ellis Mandel. They were much concerned about locating some unidentified missing property of Stompanato's. I advised them that the last address we had on him was the Del Capri Hotel in West Los Angeles, and that any personal property would be in charge of the Coroner or Public Administrator.

Somebody else evidently wanted the same mysterious property, because Stompanato's apartment had been expertly burglarized a few hours after his death was announced. At the time I was unaware of the existence of some startling material which the late playboy had cached in a small wooden box and passed for safekeeping to a third person because he did not trust his underworld associates. Later we were to discover the box.

As usually happens in police cases involving prominent names, wild reports circulated concerning events at Lana Turner's home on the night of the killing. Dozens of crank calls came to my office, most of them from women who claimed to know exactly what had happened. (For some reason, most crank calls are from women.) An enterprising attorney, disputing police findings in the case, dressed a life-sized dummy in the clothes Stompanato had worn on the murder night, and exhibited it on television to demonstrate his theory that the alleged knife marks indicated the victim had been supine when stabbed. However, nothing was ever revealed which gave us any reason to doubt our findings.

The charge against Cheryl was reduced to manslaughter after the evidence had been presented to the Juvenile Court. A Coroner's jury ruled that the girl's act had been justifiable homicide in defense of her mother. After a court hearing before Superior Judge Allen T. Lynch of Santa Monica, Cheryl was made a ward of the court and released from Juvenile Hall in custody of her grandmother.

Cheryl's release brought scores of letters into my office from the United States, Europe and South America, some of them extremely critical of the police department for "setting the girl free," or charging a cover-up." Many people confuse the police function with that of the courts. The police investigate, obtain evidence, apprehend law violators, and present the evidence and facts to the courts. The courts review the evidence and decide the disposition of the case. Where juveniles are concerned, the County's juvenile agency makes a separate investigation and recommendation to the Juvenile Court.

The decision in Cheryl's case was proper; her hostile critics were misinformed. Under California law all juvenile offenders, regardless of the nature of their crime, are heard in Juvenile Court. Her case was handled no differently from any other, but because she was the daughter of a celebrity she was held in the glare of world-wide newspaper publicity and pilloried by some. By contrast, a 17-year-old youth in our nearby San Fernando Valley killed his mother's lover when the man resorted to violence, and the public almost applauded him and regretted the necessity of putting the boy on probation. Yet Cheryl Crane had done no more and no less. Public prejudice against celebrities involved in police cases is a curious thing.

However, Cheryl had more defenders than critics. My office received 200 letters sympathetic to her. Many of them stated that this young girl had done more than all the law enforcement agencies had been able to do, in eliminating Stompanato. Other correspondents in foreign countries offered her a new home.

The most ironic angle of the Stompanato investigation was the refusal of the underworld to believe that this "tough" ex-Marine could have been killed so easily by a 14-year-old girl. He had been considered one of their best bodyguards, and it was a damaging blow to their ego.

Here's how it happened. Surprise and accident brought about tough, muscular Johnny's sudden death. The distraught child caught him off guard and the keen-edged butcher-knife took a freak slant. It slashed through his abdominal wall, liver and aorta, the latter the main artery carrying blood from the heart. Dr. Frederick Newbarr, chief county autopsy surgeon, told me that he must have died "in a matter of minutes." Even if a dozen doctors had been present they could not have saved him.

What would have happened if the knife had only scratched Stompanato? In my opinion he would then have used violence on both mother and daughter, as he had previously done to Miss Turner. My guess is that this final scene would have ended his domination of the actress, since men of his stripe fall apart when they encounter courageous resistance.

The most startling development in our post-mortem investigation has not been revealed to the public until now. An innocent individual to whom Stompanato had entrusted his little wooden box, turned it over to the police department. Inside the box, along with a revolver (.32 caliber snub-nosed), bank books, and personal papers, officers found roll-film negatives. Printed and enlarged, the negatives revealed pictures of nude women in compromising situations. Some of the pictures had apparently been taken while the victims were unaware they were being photographed, and they were recognizable. The pictures would have been a gold mine for a blackmailer.

Stompanato's unusual picture collection verified information we already had, but we made no serious attempt to pursue our investigation further. It would have been a cruel embarrassment to the victims, and would have served no legal purpose since the principal was now dead.

The total value of Stompanato's personal property after his death was listed by the Public Administrator at less than $400. Could this wooden box have been what the burglars were seeking in the dead man's apartment?

eight

A GALLERY OF

STYLISH SWINDLERS

WHEN I WAS A DETECTIVE, A RESTAURANT SWINDLER gave me an insight into the criminal world which I have not forgotten. He had a pleasant manner, and, we discovered later, a long police record, including 16 arrests for passing counterfeit money. While serving time, he had worked in prison kitchens and learned the business of food preparation. He appeared in Beverly Hills at a time when a restaurant owner was in financial trouble and wanted a partner. Three days before Thanksgiving, the swindler agreed to buy a $10,000 interest in the restaurant, and went into escrow in a neighborhood bank on a deal which, he said, would transfer $50,000 from his Chicago bank.

On Thanksgiving Day the restaurant did a tremendous business, and the owner was delighted when his new partner sent him home to rest, volunteering to stay until closing time. The partner stayed on as promised, but after closing up for the night he took all the bar receipts, totaling $1000, and skipped town. He drove all night to reach Reno, Nevada, and started gambling as soon as he arrived. He made the mistake of continuing to play after losing the $1000, and paid his further losses to the gamblers with two checks written on the Beverly Hills bank. The suspicious gamblers called the manager of the hotel where he was staying, and the latter called me long-distance to ask about his guest's financial status. I checked with the restaurant owner, who by now had discovered that both his new partner and his money were missing.

I picked the swindler up in Reno and started home with him, driving his car (which was owned by a finance company.) He was a typical ex-convict who didn't want to talk, and sat in resentful silence as the hours and miles went by. However, after I fed him a good steak dinner in a California mountain town, he opened up on his background and talked for an hour or more about his lawless life. The criminal world, I learned, is not a mysterious system, and not even organized in the usual sense of the word. In the swindler's case, he had served as a cook and waiter in several Federal penitentiaries where he met vice lords from all parts of the United States, some of whom owned restaurants. After his release it had been a simple matter for him to go from city to city, getting jobs in places owned by his former prison pals and meeting their friends. Just as church and lodge members find religious and fraternal associates whenever they move into a new community, so criminals can easily locate their kind. They don't have to have a formal connection with each other, as the Mafia is said to maintain; their association is just the common product of living outside the law.

Swindlers of all kinds have hit our city during the years, bogus stock salesmen, oil promoters, vending-machine sharpsters, fake talent schools, phoney motion-picture projects, and dozens of others, including an "insurance" group operated by four fellows with a borrowed desk, who had literature going all over the United States before the State Insurance Commissioner caught up with them.

Because confidence men seek the prestige of a Beverly

Hills address for their operations, police keep a watchful eye on strangers who use local post office boxes, mail drops, and street numbers for business enterprises, and sometimes find swindlers. In most cases they have been ex-convicts. This is one reason why the city has an ordinance requiring ex-convicts to register with the police department, if they are inside the city limits more than five times in 30 days, an ordinance which is now being tested in the higher courts for its constitutionality.

Even gypsy fortune-tellers have hit Beverly Hills, sometimes successfully. Years ago, when motion-picture stars were more naive about their money, the late Lupe Velez was victimized by an itinerant gypsy woman using the oldest bunko game in the business. Poor little Lupe, whose short and tempestuous career was to end in suicide, listened to the woman's description of an ancient gypsy ritual which would bring her good luck. The actress followed instructions carefully. She handed the woman $2500 in paper currency, which the latter put a "gypsy charm" on and handed back, wrapped in a piece of Miss Velez's silk negligee. All that the actress had to do now was to hold the package of money close to her all night, and in the morning her troubles would be over. However, when she unwrapped the silken package next morning she discovered that her paper money had been replaced by strips of wrapping paper. The volatile Mexican actress was sputtering with rage when she called the police, proclaiming she "wanted to get her hands on that woman," but the gypsy had folded her tent.

During my patrolman days I spotted a man going from store to store along Wilshire Boulevard late one evening. He had the air of a "con" man, which trained policemen can sense. After watching him enter and leave three establishments, I followed to check up on his activity. At the first two places they reported that he was looking for cab fare to Los Angeles, about $5 at that time, and offered to leave a gold watch for security. My third stop was a drug store

78

the man had visited, and the druggist's story was the same, except that he told me how he had outwitted the visitor.

"I was wise to that fellow," he confided. "I could see his gold watch wasn't worth a dime, but he had a nice ring on his finger and I gave him $10 for it. Pretty nifty, eh?" He handed me the ring with a small flourish and I looked at it. It was a very nice piece of glass. I immediately took out after the con man and arrested him before any more of my wards could take advantage of him. He had "sold" eight watches out of an original dozen, and had a pocket full of cheap rings and $100 in cash. He bought the rings and watches from an eastern novelty manufacturer by the gross, and worked his way from coast to coast unloading them on gullible citizens, who figured they were getting a rare bargain.

Twenty-five years later I still find con men pulling the same old gags, only they now have new victims. Just recently we caught a man with a gross of cheap watches and artificial pearl necklaces, which he had been peddling to buyers, who let their inborn avarice overcome their scruples. The fellow confided to his suckers that his merchandise was stolen property, and therefore he had to get rid of it at a fraction of its real value.

Since Beverly Hills is located near the ocean, another popular dodge is often tried by con men, who appear on a busy street dressed as merchant seamen—battered cap, pea jacket and turtleneck sweater—and with mock furtiveness dispose of "smuggled" furs, jewelry and perfume. Since there is an illegal tinge to the transaction, the swindlers know their dupes will probably not hurry to report to the police, when they discover they have paid good money for the cheapest kind of imitations.

Beggars would thrive in our town if the police department would permit it. Here, again, location makes us vulnerable to a hard-luck story which also carries a bogus appeal to our patriotism. Since we are situated only a few miles from Sawtelle and the Veterans Administrative Center, numerous con men appear, claiming to be stranded veterans who need bus fare to carry them back to the soldiers' home. If they want to cinch their plea, they become "disabled veterans." This story is often good for 40 or 50 cents from soft-hearted and gullible pedestrians. Frequently we have picked up such panhandlers with $50 to $60 in their pockets, gleaned from local citizens, which is a good substantial income for a few hours "work."

Bogus military men in uniform love to parade as celebrities in Beverly Hills. We've had numerous phoney officers, representing both land and sea forces of our foreign allies as well as the United States. They take rooms at one of our fine hotels, get a little publicity started, run up bills like mad, and pay them with bad checks. We generally turn these types over to the FBI or the military for disciplining. One such visitor was a "Navy officer" whose battle experiences had been so thrilling that he was in great demand as a speaker at service clubs. His story was so good that we got interested and investigated it. We discovered that he had never seen a shot fired in anger; his only connection with the war had been as a seaman aboard a merchant ship.

During my years as a detective, I learned to beware of strangers wearing fraternal emblems. This is a favorite trick of a con man to put his intended victim at ease. One of the slickest bogus stock salesmen ever to hit Beverly Hills wore the emblem of a prominent service club on his lapel. We picked him up for passing bad checks, and found he had been operating all over the United States.

Swindlers' dodges are too numerous to list. I remember the "insurance" salesman who slipped a blank check for $100, made out to Cash, in among the papers he handed to a prospect to sign; and the tennis professional who led a wealthy widow to believe she was financing the building of a tennis court, but pocketed the money himself; and the beauty-shop operator who shaved trade names off ordinary bars of soap and sold them to his customers as "special skin conditioner" at fancy prices.

80

One of the more fabulous crooks who came our way was a man from Switzerland, who got away with $200,000. He had been an employee in a Swiss import-export business, with authority to handle financial transactions around the world. During World War II, when German invasion seemed imminent, he absconded with the company's funds and shipped the money out of the country in the form of credits to South America and the United States. Eventually he settled down in a Beverly Hills apartment for the duration. The Swiss government requested his arrest, and we obliged. When we searched his apartment for the missing money we were surprised to find $10,000 in currency hidden in a false bottom under a wastepaper basket. While the Swiss government was in the process of trying to get the man extradited, the owners of the money died. They never were able to extradite him. After the war, when the frozen funds of aliens were released by the United States government, he claimed the company money as his own, and, believe it or not, he got to keep it.

Because con men who are world travelers like to use a Beverly Hills address, we frequently get requests from police in foreign cities asking whether certain tourists are authentic citizens of our town. Foreign police have often tripped up international con men in this way. However, on one occasion we were able to verify the identity of a traveling citizen explicitly. We got a query from a European city as to the authenticity of a local man who was after a wealthy heiress there. We were able to send a prompt reply, assuring them we knew the man well, since we had often had him in for questioning regarding his gambling activities. I never did hear whether or not he married the girl.

Our location in the middle of the motion-picture and television industries makes Beverly Hills a favorite hunting-ground for "talent school" swindlers, who prey on young people seeking fame and fortune in the entertainment world. I remember one so-called school here in which the partners were so crooked they couldn't trust each other. However, it was not with us long. The "faculty" got to fighting among themselves over the profits, and the school closed. Police keep a watchful eye on this type of activity here.

A church movie scheme might have paid off for a trio of promoters if they had not had a falling out. They opened handsome offices and were contacting various church leaders for funds with which to finance production of religious films. They had something for all denominations, Protestant, Catholic and Jewish. The head man, a smooth-talking, impressive fellow, represented himself as a minister of whatever denomination he was "hitting." However, one of the promoters came to my office to complain that his partner was an ex-convict; and a second member informed me that the partner had threatened to kill him. I discovered that all three had police records, and we speeded their departure from the city before they collected much money.

Not many years ago, I had a nationally-known gambler and ex-convict in my office for an investigation. I had been told he was trying to negotiate card games with wealthy men, and had taken a rich Kern County oil man for $100,000. He was also attempting to raise money for a steamship line which appeared questionable. However, the gambler was too cagey to admit anything. Next day his wife descended on my office threatening civil action. She wanted me to know that her husband was a reliable citizen and not a confidence man, and that she herself was extremely wealthy and prepared to spend her money to stop this harassment of her husband. Furthermore, she was related to the Governor of an eastern State who could make things hot for me.

At this time Mr. and Mrs. Gambler lived in a large house in an expensive section of the city and were socially active. However, after our talks, his attempts to finance his shipping venture ceased, and a short time later the couple moved away from Beverly Hills.

A friendly little old lady has extracted money from a number of citizens in our community and elsewhere with a hoax that is so simple it is amusing. She reads the society pages of newspapers carefully, looking for announcements of out-of-town weddings involving members of Beverly Hills families. Some time later, the local relatives will get a call from her announcing that she is the aunt of the lovely girl back East who married their son, or nephew, or cousin, and is on a cross-country trip. She will be here for one day only, stopping at a downtown Los Angeles hotel, and would just love to see them.

Naturally, our hospitable Californians rush down to the hotel, pick up Aunt Mamie, or whatever name she uses, and take her for a tour of the city, and to lunch at the Farmer's Market, and have a wonderful time talking about the wedding. Eventually, Aunt Mamie confides that she lost part of her money somewhere along the way, and will have to cut her trip short although she had been looking forward to a day in San Francisco before returning home. Of course, her new friends, almost relatives-by-marriage, insist on lending her $50 or more immediately to be repaid after she gets home. (Sometimes they cash a check for her.) At this point, Aunt Mamie decides she would like to return to her hotel and rest before resuming her journey. They take her back to the hotel, she waves good-bye to them from the sidewalk and walks into the lobby.

Later, when the thought occurs to them that their son has never mentioned his wife's Aunt Mamie, they begin to wonder. They call the hotel to check up on their visitor, and find that the sweet little old lady was never registered there. They probably will never see her again, but the police will. She has been arrested numerous times in various cities, including Beverly Hills. When we arrested her and sent out teletype information, several cities were interested. After each sentence she serves she comes out and starts her little act in a new location. Come to think of it as I write this, she's about due here.

Forgers also like the climate and the money in Southern California. I remember a clever check artist who worked as night auditor at a swank night club on the Sunset Strip, between Beverly Hills and Los Angeles. One of his victims

83

was Jack Haley, the stage and screen star, who noticed, in his monthly bank statements, checks which he had apparently signed made out to "Cash" for substantial sums. Since the actor was positive he had not written any checks to "Cash" Mr. Haley came to us. Our investigation disclosed that the auditor at the club was copying the signatures of prominent patrons, forging their names on other checks on the victim's bank. Since he had all night to review the signatures, he did an expert job of it, and the forgeries were accepted as genuine by the banks.

After the forger was arrested, he got out on bail and skipped to Daytona Beach, Florida, where his once-wealthy family formerly wintered. I found him there, staying with friends, and returned him to California for sentencing. We never did know exactly how many checks he forged, but the number was considerable because in his job he had access to many of the most prominent signatures in Hollywood.

One of our bad-check artists claimed to be descended from Russian nobility and tried to get out of his financial difficulties by disappearing. He left a quantity of blood in the bathroom, and a suicide note, to discourage searchers. We lost contact with him for several months, until one day I chanced in at an attorney's office and saw a man with a full beard sitting there. It was the bad-check nobleman in a bushy disguise. I recognized the would-be Count from photographs and addressed him directly by name. He was so surprised he responded, and I took him to jail for booking and a shave.

Fake suicides are often used by people who are out to deceive. I remember a man who left his clothes and a suicide note on the shore of Lake Erie. Every indication was that he had drowned himself, leaving his grieving wife and children dependent on the State of New York for aid. However, he came to California, married another woman, and was working for a public utility company in Beverly Hills when we located him. He was arrested and returned to New York

84

State, charged with failure to provide, defrauding the State of New York, and bigamy.

The police are in the unique position of knowing socially and financially prominent individuals who in former days were in trouble with the law, such as a onetime gambler and police character who got rich as a result of fortunate oil investments and became a society figure.

I have also known young men who had brushes with the law for forgery, bad checks and minor offenses, who in later years became community leaders. When I was a detective we had a group of three young fellows who migrated here from the East and put on a big front by passing worthless checks. They shared a nice apartment and a sporty automobile, and were active in Hollywood party life. However, a finance company repossessed their car almost every 60 days, and other creditors pursued them.

After looking for one of the trio for some time on a bad-check charge, I spotted him dining in a swanky restaurant with a gorgeous girl from out of town. I tapped him on the shoulder and put him under arrest. He was a handsome sportsman and a lion in cafe society, but when he left the table to accompany me to jail he didn't have enough money to pay the bill. The girl had to pay it for him.

Maybe the arrest marked the turning-point in the life of this young man and his playboy pals. All three later became successful business and professional men and valuable citizens of our community. One is a big man in aviation, another is an important motion-picture executive, and my ex-prisoner can write a check for $500,000 and it won't bounce—today.

nine

SOCIETY

RACKETEERS

A WOMAN NAMED MRS. VIVIAN LINGLE, LOADED WITH personality and a police record, was a big-time operator in Beverly Hills social circles. Her ability to organize "benefits", and enlist the services of prominent women as fund-raisers, was really astonishing. She had the brass of a burglar. When we once refused her a permit, under terms of a city ordinance which requires charity solicitors to register, she made a dramatic appearance before the City Council and raised Cain in an attempt to get our ruling reversed. Yet we knew at the time, as did she, that her scheme was just another racket in which the dollars would go to her, and the pennies to charity.

She had been identified with money-raising projects for many years, and met many important people. During World War II, she made her local debut as one of the active leaders of the Women's Emergency Corps, and got prominent women to serve on the board of directors. The group formally disbanded in 1946, but Mrs. Lingle kept right on using its name. In 1953 she came up with a plan to raise money for the benefit of wounded veterans of the Korean war, and their families, by selling chances on a new Cadillac sedan. She had stacks of tickets printed, listing the Corps as sponsor, and, with the help of her society volunteers, sold several thousand of them at $1 each. However, the plan had one flaw which aroused the curiosity of the police; there was no Cadillac.

After we arrested her we discovered she had also forged the name of Mrs. Alice Cooper, mother of Gary Cooper, in endorsing and cashing checks which had been sent to the defunct Women's Emergency Corps, among them contributions from Bing Crosby and the late Ronald Coleman. And we found 10,000 more tickets for the Cadillac in the apartment of her partner. Their overhead on this little deal, which netted them more than $6000 before the police stepped in, was a total of $50.

Mrs. Lingle had another dodge which was also a beauty. Knowing that there were many veterans recovering from wounds in nearby military hospitals, she approached automobile dealers and borrowed new cars to give the veterans rides. However, in each instance she would fail to return the automobile. Some dealers waited as long as two months, and finally had to find her and take back their property. But nobody could have her arrested, because she had permission to use the cars.

Nothing was too good for the veterans—or Mrs. Lingle. She established a nice apartment which, she said, was for the use of returning war veterans and their long-separated wives, and prevailed on the women of Beverly Hills to furnish and equip the place in fine style, and then lived in it herself. There was nothing secretive about her. She let the donors inspect the apartment, invited them in for parties at which liquor and champagne flowed, and raised more money to keep the scheme going. The apartment, furnishings, liquor and food, of course, were obtained by fraudulent representation that they were for a veterans' organization.

She lived high at the best hotels for several years on

money she collected for veterans, and always had a list of wealthy people she could touch for more when funds ran low. After her arrest, she faced a penitentiary sentence, but on the day she was supposed to appear in court she failed to show up. A search was made for her, and she was found dead in her Los Angeles apartment, a suicide.

Through the years, promoters have harvested hundreds of thousands of dollars in Beverly Hills in the name of youth, veterans, hospitals and other philanthropic and charitable causes. We now screen all fund-raising projects through a Social Welfare Committee to prevent unscrupulous individuals from victimizing our citizens, and we have uncovered a number of so-called charity drives in which the promoters get the larger share of the receipts and the charity gets only whatever small percentage is left over. Frequently "donations" are made by buying chances on an expensive automobile, thus circumventing the laws prohibiting raffles. In one such operation which hit Beverly Hills, we found that many thousands of tickets had been sold throughout California and neighboring States—for just one automobile!

Fund-raising for philanthropic purposes is one of the biggest businesses nationally, with total receipts in the billion-dollar bracket several times over. The public is more susceptible to a charitable appeal than any other, and often accepts without investigation the statements made by promoters whose hearts bleed for their fellowmen.

Because Beverly Hills is both charitable and wealthy, and lures all types of operators raising money, our ordinance regulating such activities is strictly enforced. Only recently a magazine promoter and two solicitors were sentenced to 120 days in jail for soliciting funds here without a permit. They were raising money for a publication to be devoted to law enforcement agencies which deal with juvenile delinquency. They appealed all the way to the United States Supreme Court, which upheld our ordinance.

Our purpose is not to handicap legitimate charities. In 1958, for example, the Social Welfare Committee granted

66 permits and rejected only 15 which failed to meet minimum requirements. However, every year since the committee has been in existence, the number of applications for permits has declined. Applicants know that extensive investigation will be made before a permit is granted, and our investigators have uncovered many rackets.

One slick deal which turned up was a "Veterans' Post," organized by half-a-dozen men who went into the salvage business, temporarily, picking up a nice haul of discarded furniture and clothing from well-to-do homes. The "post" also sold tickets for a benefit dance for hospitalized veterans, but all the legitimate veterans received from this scheme was two small radio sets.

A bogus religious leader, who wore what looked like a Salvation Army cap, with the wording on it illegible, gave us considerable trouble. We found him going from door to door soliciting funds. Officers had warned him away several times, but he persisted in his canvassing. He was brought to headquarters, where he indignantly made a speech on religious freedom, implying that the Beverly Hills Police Department was hindering the work of the Almighty. I explained that we never interfered with bona-fide religious activity, but were concerned only with fraud.

He finally consented to fill out an application blank for a permit, giving the address of his church. We found it to be a small store building in South Los Angeles, with a piano and a dozen chairs in it. Our subject's religious work was limited to a Sunday School he conducted for a few kids on Sabbath mornings, leaving him free to collect funds the rest of the week. He had been doing very well at it. He had purchased considerable business property in his own name, and organized a company with a 14-year-old girl as secretary-treasurer, and a woman friend as vice-president. He also had a police record on morals charges. When we advised him of our findings he gave us no more trouble.

Another beautiful scheme was dreamed up by a man and his wife who collected funds to care for old dogs who had outlived their usefulness. They charged their clients $25 each to make a home for the family pet during its declining years. This racket had a sure-fire appeal to animal lovers, who couldn't bear to think of having old Rover put away, and was particularly good in Beverly Hills where some 3500 dogs live in near-luxury. To convince customers of their genuine love for pets, the man and his wife were active leaders in the anti-vivisection campaign in Southern California. The only catch in this humanitarian project was that the slickers, after collecting the dogs, took them to a neighboring city, where they disposed of them either by sale or by turning them in at the city pound.

Con men have something for everybody, and this one got the dog-lovers until the police found out about it. Nobody dares raise his voice against man's best friend, as a nationally famous actor realized recently when he called headquarters to complain about a barking dog that was keeping him awake. "Please make him shut up—but don't use my name!" he said. "I'm a public figure and I've got to *love* dogs!"

One promoter representing a fraternal order sold 3500 tickets for a benefit performance at a theater with 2000 seats. But his advertising was too good. Much to his dismay, almost all the ticket holders showed up at the theater, and a small riot resulted when there were no seats for many of them.

Since our wealthy citizens are always looking for expensive and famous art objects for their homes, police keep a watchful eye on estate auctions. We visited one such sale, advertised as "from the estate of Rudolph Valentino," and could find only two items, among rooms full of paintings, furniture, antiques and what not, that had ever belonged to "The Great Lover." Everything else had been brought in from outside. Another auctioneer announced he had a fine group of original paintings by Rosa Bonheur, Degas, Dufy, Manet and others, all from "a prominent Beverly Hills estate." Since the value of these, if genuine, would have been hundreds of thousands of dollars, local art dealers investigated and reported to police that all was not kosher. We arrested the auctioneer for misleading advertising, and he was found guilty after a long trial filled with expert testimony. He appealed, but the verdict was upheld, resulting in a fine for the auctioneer.

Police are always on the alert for telephone salesmen with unusual projects. We spoiled the game of one who was calling residents to solicit subscriptions for a phoney "blue book" of local society. Another man was selling ads for a magazine which, he said, was sponsored by a political party. We found that no such publication was planned by the party, and arrested him. As often happens in such swindles, he was an ex-convict. After 30 years on the force I have learned most of the tricks of con men, yet they continue to flourish in spite of the many warnings which the police department and the Better Business Bureau give the public.

The late Elmer Perry and his Beverly Hills Athletic Club were a police problem for several years. Perry was a smooth operator. Outwardly he appeared to be a public benefactor and philanthropist, but actually he was a wolf out to fleece the sheep. A professional gambler, he established the club as a front for his illegal activities, but he permitted civic, fraternal and religious organizations to rent the main room of the club for a nominal fee and thereby won the friendship of many leading citizens.

What his friendly guests did not know was that he ran a big-time gambling operation in the back room, frequented by such steady customers as Bugsy Siegel and Al Smiley, and that the club was also a contact spot for the gambling ship, *Lux*, which the late Tony Cornero operated offshore during the 1940s. On one occasion, at the annual dinner of a wealthy civic organization, somebody started a crap game, and two "ringers," both experienced gamblers, took all the money. But Perry's unsuspecting guests didn't realize they had been taken.

The front part of the club was respectable; the action was all in the back. Perry would gather a dozen men in the back room at 10 or 11 P.M. for poker games, and the "pros" naturally got most of the money. We learned about these shady doings at the club when one of the suckers complained to the police department. We watched the club and raided it on a night when Perry and his pals were having a big game. We arrested 12 persons for gambling, 11 of them with police records, and found that two of the players were former members of the Purple Gang in Detroit. Under the table, police found two revolvers, and booked the men on suspicion of robbery as well.

Perry was found guilty and fined, but he never gave up in his campaign to win influential public support. Each year when a new City Council took office, Perry would appear before it and complain of police harassment of his harmless social club, and we would patiently point out that it harbored gamblers.

We tried to take away his liquor license by notifying the State Board of Equalization of Perry's sinister activities, but he fought this move with letters of glowing recommendation from service clubs, and political and religious groups which used the premises for their meetings. A powerful political organization's letter avowed that Perry never sold liquor after 2 A.M., or to minors; a rabbi praised the club's "atmosphere of refinement" for meetings and weddings; and a priest lauded its physical culture facilities and the cooperation given by the management in providing a place for church charity bazaars. We were outnumbered and outmaneuvered! However, we continued our strict surveillance of the club until Perry sold it to a group of reputable business people who operated it legitimately.

A few years later, Elmer Perry was killed in gangland fashion near the La Brea tar pits in Los Angeles. There was a lot of speculation concerning his death, and other gamblers were suspected, since he had a reputation as an adept card shark. Some years afterwards I was astonished to learn that a prominent motion-picture director, well-known in sporting circles, had financed the activities at Perry's club, and that a former member of my department had been connected with it. However, the man had been dismissed from the force for other irregularities before I made this discovery. Once again the Perry affair demonstrated to me the ease with which smooth-talking con men can hoodwink many reputable citizens, who will then personally vouch for them as character witnesses.

"Friendly" card games for housewives drained off considerable household funds in Beverly Hills before the police got wise to the operations of two women card sharks. This conniving couple would meet housewives at markets, or in neighborhood social events, and suggest they get together a group of their friends for card games at small stakes. It was all very gay and clubby, but at the end of these pleasant afternoon sessions the innocent housewives had no money. Occasionally police are criticized for raiding card games, but, believe me, they have the public's best interests at heart. Such protection is essential to unsuspecting victims of card sharks.

We once had a "wealthy European financier" who supported himself for several months in an expensive hotel suite by playing cards. When the police caught up with him we discovered he was nothing more nor less than a professional gambler who had learned how to play cards in the game rooms at Reno.

A gin rummy scandal rocked the movie colony in the late 1930s, when it was rumored that two young men from prominent families were winning large sums of money with suspicious regularity. Their victims included a celebrated motion-picture producer, who dropped $30,000 before he decided he couldn't play gin rummy with experts. A Chicago business executive, here for a vacation, left town $200,000 poorer after tangling with the local players.

At this time a gin rummy "craze" was widespread, comparable to the canasta fad of the 1950s. Everybody was playing it. Smart hostesses planned their parties so that gin rummy fanatics could have long evenings around the card tables, and the games continued on week-ends at beach and country clubs, and at Malibu, Lake Arrowhead and Palm Springs.

Inevitably, some card sharks with good social connections moved in and began collecting heavily from movie celebrities and other wealthy citizens. Nobody complained to the police, however, because everybody could afford to lose; some of the losers even bragged about it. Two gin rummy players on a Los Angeles-to-Chicago train found an easy "pigeon" in a Beverly Hills business man. They let him win a few games on the train, then renewed the play in a Chicago hotel room and took him for $3000. Another citizen tried to match his skill with some expert players in a city park. He won $200 on the first day but on subsequent days as the game continued he lost $1800.

The two young con men who fleeced their friends and acquaintances in the movie colony were never reported to the police, since they limited their games to private homes. However, a memorable dinner party at the home of Cobina Wright, Beverly Hills social leader and newspaper columnist, exposed their activities. Mrs. Wright invited the cream of Hollywood society to her home for the evening, "big-name" stars and top executives of the studios. Clark Gable, Charlie Chaplin, Lana Turner, Paulette Goddard and Walter Pidgeon were among the crowd of celebrities who attended. I was invited as a representative of the police department.

After dinner, Mrs. Wright introduced two unusually interesting guests. One was the late Raymond Schindler, nationally-famous private detective; the other was a former vaudeville performer and card-trick magician named Mc-Dougall, who had been hired by steamship lines and railroads to catch gin rummy sharks, who were preying on wealthy travelers. Mr. Schindler spoke to the guests on the subject of card sharks and the fortune they were reaping as a result of the popularity of gin rummy, a game which is admirably suited to their trickery.

After Mr. Schindler's talk he turned the meeting over to McDougall who gave a demonstration exposing the method of operation of the gin rummy sharks. With the help of Miss Turner and Miss Goddard, who were his "pigeons" in an exhibition game, McDougall showed how easily an expert can stack a gin rummy deck. Even without stacking, expert players can know the location of almost every card after one or two hands have been played. A "pigeon" in such a game never has a chance.

It was all handled very politely, and no names were mentioned, but from that time on the depredations of the Hollywood card sharks dwindled.

ten

I REMEMBER

WALBURGA

THE NAME OF MRS. WALBURGA OESTERREICH HAS FADED from public memory, but not from mine. I used to see her frequently when I was a rookie patrolman on Wilshire Boulevard. She was a middle-aged widow, living in seclusion in an apartment over a large and handsome super-market which she owned. It was the first such establishment in Beverly Hills.

My beat took me past the market twice a day, and my normal professional interest in the property was whetted by the circumstance that its owner was at this time in the headlines as a key figure in the most fantastic murder story I had ever encountered. Yet somehow I could never mentally link the stolid, silent woman I saw there with the strange events in her life, and certainly not with "the ghost of the garret."

Occasionally stories come to light in real life which are far more improbable than any in fiction. Such was the ordeal of Walburga Oesterreich.

It had begun years before, on an August night in 1922,

when a series of shots and a woman's scream shattered the midnight quiet of an exclusive Los Angeles neighborhood. Police, arriving on the scene, found the body of Fred Oesterreich, a wealthy apron manufacturer, lying on the floor of his living-room. The body had been neatly punctured by three bullets from a .25 caliber automatic pistol, fired at close range. Two bullets had penetrated near his heart and a third in the back of his head.

The expensively furnished room showed evidence of a fierce struggle. Heavy rugs had been shoved and twisted, a table cover had been pulled off on the floor, and a chair overturned across the body. An open French window, with screen unlatched, suggested that the murderer had left the house hurriedly.

There was no sign of the victim's wife downstairs, although neighbors reported they had heard her arguing with her husband when the couple arrived home earlier in the evening. Searching the upstairs, detectives heard a scream from a bedroom closet. They tried to open the door, but it had been locked from the outside. The key was missing.

Somebody found the key where it had been dropped on the hallway floor. The police unlocked the closet door and discovered Mrs. Oesterreich, weeping and hysterical.

She told her rescuers she had been standing in the closet hanging up her coat when she heard a violent commotion downstairs and the sound of shots. She had started to leave the closet to investigate, but as she did so someone had slammed the door shut and locked it. Then she had screamed.

The widow accompanied the officers on a tour of the premises. Everything seemed to be in place, except for her husband's valuable diamond-studded wristwatch which was missing. Apparently he had been shot and killed by burglars, who had been frightened away by his brave resistance.

Detectives wondered, however, why any burglar would be carrying such a dainty weapon as a .25 caliber automatic, a gun more likely to be found in a lady's purse. They also puzzled over the report of a next-door neighbor, who said she had peered through her window after the shooting and seen a man walk through the Oesterreich living-room, and that later somebody inside the house had turned off the porch light.

For almost a year it was generally believed that burglars had killed Mr. Oesterreich. Then a hard working Los Angeles detective, Captain Herman Cline, blew the burglary theory sky high. He discovered the missing wristwatch in possession of the attorney who was settling the apron-maker's estate. When Captain Cline questioned the widow about this curious development she explained that she had found the watch at home some months after the murder. She had not considered it important enough to bother the police about. Besides, she didn't want to stir up a lot of publicity.

The discovery of the wristwatch resulted in so much furor in the newspapers that two men, almost simultaneously, walked into Los Angeles police headquarters with identical stories. Each had disposed of a small-caliber automatic pistol for Mrs. Oesterreich, at her request. One man had tossed his gun into the La Brea tar pits on Wilshire Boulevard, and the other had buried his weapon under a rose bush at home. Police recovered both guns but found the identification numbers had been obliterated by exposure.

Once again the police closely questioned Mrs. Oesterreich. She explained that the guns were old things she had kept around the house for many years but never used. She had decided to get rid of them because, under the circumstances of her husband's death, their presence in her home might prove embarrassing.

Within an hour the widow was lodged in jail and charged with murder. Things looked bleak for her, but she was not destined to stay behind bars for long. She became ill while awaiting trial, after a brief preliminary hearing, and was released on $50,000 bail. Meanwhile the District Attorney's investigators hacked away tirelessly at her story, but without success. There was just no flaw in it. She repeatedly reminded them that police officers had found her *inside* the closet after the shooting, with the door locked from the *outside*.

Months later, after they had tested and discarded every possible theory which might link her to the crime, the investigators admitted defeat and the murder complaint against the widow was dismissed.

Seven years passed, and the Oesterreich murder had been all but forgotten when a surprising new development brought it back into the headlines. In April, 1930, an attorney formerly employed by Mrs. Oesterreich revealed to the authorities the existence of a "bat man" who had lived in the Oesterreich attic at the time of the murder and was ready to confess. The attorney led police to Otto Sanhuber, a rather small, quiet man in horn-rimmed glasses, who was working as a janitor in a Los Angeles apartment house.

While the amazed police listened, Sanhuber unfolded an incredible story of having lived for more than 10 years as "the ghost of the garret" in the Oesterreich household.

It had all started in Milwaukee, he said, when he was a young sewing machine mechanic in Mr. Oesterreich's apron factory. Dolly, as he called Mrs. Oesterreich, had taken a liking to him and he became a friend of the family. At first he had been popular with Mr. Oesterreich, too, until he took a trip to St. Louis with Dolly, after which a certain coolness was observed in her husband's attitude toward Otto. Mr. Oesterreich, in fact, ordered Otto to get lost and stay away from both his door and his Dolly.

Mrs. Oesterreich, working on another leg of the triangle, came up with an idea which solved the whole situation and set up a murder: she secretly installed Otto in her attic. From then on, wherever the Oesterreichs lived, Otto went along and set up housekeeping under Walburga's roof without the husband being any the wiser.

Altogether, Sanhuber ticked off four attics in Milwaukee and three in Los Angeles before the murder ended his rent free existence. When the family moved to Los Angeles in 1918, Otto had wanted to get out and join the Army because there was a war going on. Mrs. Oesterreich, while perhaps impressed with his patriotism wouldn't hear of it. She had just found a California house with a fine attic.

The newspapers quickly dubbed Otto a "love slave." Every morning, after the straight man of the house left for work among the aprons, Sanhuber would descend from his garret hideway and help Mrs. Oesterreich with her housework. He made beds, cleaned house, scrubbed vegetables, and was generally useful during the day. He lived on scraps of food left in the kitchen. At night he would steal back into his attic and read newspapers and magazines by candlelight until bedtime. Sometimes Mrs. Oesterreich would join him him there, he said. (When police later checked his story they found old periodicals, bedding and candlewax drippings in his former garret home.)

On the night of the shooting, he said, he heard the Oesterreichs quarreling downstairs, and the noise of a tussle. He took a gun, one of a pair he had owned for years, and crawled out of the attic to go to the aid of Dolly. When he reached the foot of the stairs he saw that she had been knocked to the floor. Oesterreich recognized Sanhuber and for the few seconds he had to live must have been one of the most surprised cuckolds in the country. Enraged, he charged the cowering Sanhuber, yelling, "What are you doing here, you——." Three slugs fired in panic at point blank range dropped Oesterreich dead at their feet.

Sanhuber said he then forced Mrs. Oesterreich to go upstairs, and locked her in the closet to make the shooting look like the work of burglars. Afterwards he climbed back into his attic, and hid there while police, who had been summoned by neighbors, searched the house. Some months later he gave her his guns to dispose of, he said.

Although Sanhuber's confession seemed to clear Mrs. Oesterreich she was, nevertheless, indicted for murder along with him, and again placed in County Jail.

Sanhuber revised his story on the witness stand at his trial. In his new version he said an unknown intruder had

100

done the killing, and he had confessed only to save Dolly from further exbarrassment. However, the prosecutor read the "bat man's" confession to the jury which proceeded to find him guilty of manslaughter.

Then came the final twist in this freak case. Because the statutes of limitation outlaw the crime of manslaughter after seven years, Sanhuber could not be punished for a crime committed eight years before. Although he was convicted, he went free.

Mrs. Oesterreich then was put on trial in Superior Court, charged with complicity in the murder. Her defense was skillfully handled by Jerry Giesler, a Beverly Hills citizen who is now probably America's best known criminal lawyer. Tearfully she testified that Otto had in fact shot her husband, but that she had not told the truth about the killing earlier because it was just too embarrassing to talk about her unique housekeeping arrangement with shy little Otto. She had only been an innocent bystander at her husband's death, and was in no wise involved in the crime.

The widow Walburga's trial continued for a month, with press and public hanging on every bizarre word of testimony. It ended with a hung jury, which was discharged after a three-day deadlock. A new trial date was set, but before that day arrived the District Attorney's office threw in the sponge and asked the court to dismiss the indictment. The D.A. said it was simply impossible to find enough evidence to warrant another trial.

Freed from the cloud which had hung over her for eight years, Mrs. Oesterreich retired immediately to the seclusion of her Beverly Hills apartment and to the management of her Wilshire Boulevard real estate. Otto Sanhuber also faded from public view and was never heard from again. Yet whenever oldtimers locally reminisce about bizarre murder cases, somebody always brings up the story of the "ghost of the garret."

Another famous Beverly Hills citizen, whose life was changed by a sensational murder case, came under my protective eye in the early days. She was Mary Miles Minter, a once beautiful star of motion pictures, whose interior decorating shop on Santa Monica Boulevard catered to the carriage trade in our city.

Her bright career as an actress had ended abruptly in 1922, following the unsolved murder of William Desmond Taylor, a leading motion picture director, with whom she had been friendly. Although Miss Minter was never involved in the crime, her friendship for the murdered man was played up in the press. When a nation-wide storm of condemnation and criticism of Hollywood arose over this and other sensational cases, during the investigation of the murder, she quit the screen.

It was an abrupt ending for a career which had promised much. She had been brought from New York to Hollywood with a million-dollar contract before she was 17 years old. No teen-age actress today commands such a spectacular salary, even in our cheaper dollars. For the young and beautiful star, then, to give up fame and fortune must have been a shattering experience. Yet when I used to see her on my daily rounds she was a quiet, pleasant woman, who went about her business of decorating some of the finer homes in our city, apparently with no regrets for the past, and never speaking of her misfortune.

It takes all kinds of people to make a city and a policeman's memoirs. In Beverly Hills, one of our really interesting characters was Tony Cornero, a retired rum-runner who switched to gambling after the repeal of prohibition put him out of the bootlegging business. Tony was not above making an honest dollar, too, and for several years operated a legitimate ocean freighting line.

Although Tony's gambling activities caused considerable excitement elsewhere, inside the limits of Beverly Hills he conducted himself as circumspectly as any other taxpayer. He lived with his wife and elderly mother, in a small house on a quiet street, and gave our police department no trouble except for one unfortunate incident when an unknown gunman bungled an assassination of Cornero at the door of his

102

home. Tony was badly wounded and lost a prodigious amount of blood but would never tell me who did it.

A stocky, granite-faced man with piercing grey eyes, Tony's trademark was a broad-brimmed Stetson hat jammed down over his ears. His full name was Tony Cornero Stralla, but he liked to be known as Cornero.

He had got his start in the early 1920s when, with shotgun in hand, he hijacked contraband liquor from rum-runners trying to land their cargo by night on Southern California beaches. Within a few years Tony himself was "King of the Rum-runners," and reportedly made $1,000,000 in his illicit enterprise before he was 30. Aggressive and intelligent, he was a big-time operator who led Federal officers a fast chase from the Mexican to Canadian borders.

In 1926, he put 4000 cases of liquor aboard the *S.S. Lilly* at Vancouver, British Columbia, and transported it to a point 150 miles off the coast of Southern California, where he held the ship while motor launches unloaded it and hauled its valuable cargo ashore.

He was the hero of a cops-and-robbers chase shortly thereafter. Enroute to Seattle by train, presumably to arrange another Canadian liquor deal, Tony evaded Federal officers by leaping from the train in Northern California. He hired an airplane to fly him to a point near Portland, Oregon, and caught the same train again. When the pursuing prohibition agents closed in on him again, he jumped from the train a second time, near Seattle, and made his way safely to Canada.

From Canada, Tony went to Europe and South America, and wherever he turned up there were stories of big deals. In Hamburg, Germany, he reportedly purchased the *S.S. Prezmysl* and sent it to sea with a $1,000,000 cargo of liquor for thirsty Americans, however the liquor was never traced here.

After three years of exile, Tony inexplicably returned to California and gave himself up to Federal authorities. He entered the Federal prison at McNeil Island and served a two-year sentence for smuggling liquor.

Nothing more was heard of Tony until 1938 when the

gambling ship, *Rex,* anchored three-and-a-half miles offshore in Santa Monica Bay and invited visitors aboard to gamble, dine and dance. It was equipped with slot machines, dice tables, roulette wheels, blackjack outfits, and the best of liquors served in an air of opulence as impressive as any of the Sunset Strip nightspots. There was also an orchestra for dinner dancing. It was a unique, $200,000 floating casino, and the man in command was Tony Cornero of Beverly Hills.

Public response was enthusiastic. Hundreds of Angelenos, and probably some citizens of Beverly Hills, flocked aboard to throw their money on Tony's gaming tables. When Santa Monica police and Los Angeles County officers raided the pleasure barge and arrested his customers, Tony protested that he was beyond the three-mile limit and outside the jurisdiction of the county. He moved his pleasure barge out 12 miles and kept on gambling, in defiance of State and local officials.

For more than a year crowds gambled on the *Rex,* and on three other barges which joined "Admiral" Cornero's fleet, anchored off Long Beach and Santa Monica. Finally a combined task force of shore authorities boarded and closed three of the gambling ships, in August, 1939. But the *Rex,* with Tony personally in command, refused to strike its colors. Tony barricaded the gangway with heavy steel doors and held off the enemy boarding party in a nine-day skirmish. His deckhands kept the officers' boats at bay by playing streams of water overside from three heavy fire hoses.

Tony claimed his ship was in international waters outside the jurisdiction of the United States, and hurled the threat that if this harassment did not cease he just might hoist the Japanese flag.

The "battle of Santa Monica Bay" ended four months later when Tony abandoned ship and surrendered in compliance with an abatement order served by Attorney-General Earl Warren of California, now Chief Justice of the United States Supreme Court. Tony was allowed to keep the ship, but officers destroyed all the gambling equipment—120 slot

104

machines, 20 dice tables, 20 roulette wheels, 25 blackjack tables and other illegal paraphernalia by the simple expedient of heaving everything overboard. Later, according to the story Tony told me, he lost the *Rex* to his three ex-partners in a 20-hour crap game.

In 1946 the dauntless Tony was back at sea again in a new gambling ship, the *S.S. Lux*, a former Navy mine-layer which he had converted at a cost of $150,000. Anchored off Long Beach, the *Lux* had all the latest gambling equipment, plus daytime horse-race betting, with results flashed to the ship by short-wave radio. Elmer Perry, a Beverly Hills gambler, was one of Tony's partners in the ship, which had a maritime license to operate in coastal trade.

However, the *Lux* had a short unhappy life. The Coast Guard claimed it was not in coastal trade and seized it as a menace to navigation soon after Tony opened it for business. Once again slot machines, dice tables, roulette wheels, birdcages and other gambling equipment were dumped overboard, and the *S.S. Lux* became the center of a series of court battles.

Meanwhile, Tony retreated hastily into the legitimate shipping business, operating small coastal freighters carrying bananas, lumber and beef between Pacific Coast ports. He also sniffed a chance to make some quick money in Mexico and became active in plans to reopen gambling there. Other American gamblers were understandably unhappy over Cornero's plans. Thus it happened that one night, as he was conferring with two Mexican officials in his Beverly Hills home, Tony was called to the front door by a messenger who said he had an important package for him. Hidden behind the package was a revolver, and a single bullet from it struck down Tony when he opened the door.

There were many guesses as to what the shooting was about, but when I questioned Tony he never dropped even a hint. One theory was that the gunman was trying to hold up Cornero and grab the payoff money he supposedly had in the house; another was that Tony was shot by agents of another gambling group bidding for Mexican concessions. However, it is almost impossible for police to solve shooting scrapes among the mobsters because the victims never talk and will not identify suspects. True to the code, Tony insisted he had never seen the gunman before, and didn't have an enemy in the world who would want to shoot him.

I can recall only one other police visit at Tony's home. On this occasion his wife, Mrs. Jeanne Stralla, was found to have sustained a gunshot wound which she said was accidental. There was some doubt as to who had pulled the trigger, but her story was convincing and her recovery was quick.

Tony suffered a financial reverse when one of his ships, the *S.S. Salina Cruz*, a 1300-ton lumber schooner loaded with lumber and foodstuffs for Honolulu, burned and sank off the coast of Washington in 1949. The 17 crewmen were rescued. However, as long as he could fall back on gambling Tony never seemed to worry about money. His favorite pigeons were wealthy men who thought they knew how to play poker. Tony would invite them into a little game at high stakes— and Tony usually won.

Tony died with his gambling boots on, and in style, while he was in the middle of the biggest deal of his life. He had master-minded plans for a new casino and hotel at Las Vegas to be financed by sale of stock to the public. It was to be the largest resort there, the Stardust Hotel, with 1502 rooms. The total cost would be more than $6,000,000.

In typical gambler's style, Tony got in over his head and needed money. And the fastest way he knew of getting it was gambling. Tony was rolling nicely for high stakes in Las Vegas but the dice were loaded by the master gambler no one ever beats. He collapsed at the crap table and was dead of a heart attack at 60. They counted $800 in his pockets when he died, but his estate was not large enough to cover his $3500 funeral bill.

eleven

THE BUTLER

DID IT

BUTLERS WERE PLENTIFUL IN BEVERLY HILLS IN THE days of luxury living, and some of them got into mischief in the mansions.

This is not to disparage the honest butlers who are still in service. Since World War II, they have been a vanishing species. Local domestic help not in the armed forces flocked into shipyards, aircraft factories and other war plants in the early 1940s to earn high wages as defense workers, and few of them ever returned to their former jobs in the kitchens, garages and gardens of Beverly Hills.

In earlier days many estates here had butlers, cooks, maids, chauffeurs and gardeners. Today fewer than 25 citizens employ large household staffs, among them oldtime movie stars like Marion Davies and Harold Lloyd, who made their first millions when low income taxes permitted them to keep some of the money. High income taxes, social security laws, and higher wages for domestics have forced a change in the living habits of our wealthy residents.

I was never too surprised when an errant butler made off with some of his employer's valuables, but I was amazed at the carelessness which made such pilfering possible. A bank president who spends hours checking into the character and references of a new teller will hire a domestic servant almost casually. The teller works in a gilded cage where it is practically impossible for him to steal a dime undetected; the servant, however, is turned loose in the banker's home without close supervision and with unlimited opportunities for thievery. This blind spot in wealthy and otherwise prudent householders would be amusing were it not that during the years it has been a pesky problem for the police.

I once had to track down a movie colony butler who had carted off wholesale quantities of goods from the homes of Mary Astor and the late Lupe Velez. Miss Velez, the "Mexican fireball," was the first to discover the loss at her North Rodeo Drive residence and telephoned for the police. When I learned that she employed a houseman, I started my investigation with him as the first suspect.

Another detective and I trailed the man to his apartment on West Eleventh Street in Los Angeles that night and waited until he was safely bedded down. We made an unceremonious entrance into his bedroom at 2 A.M. and woke him up. I never saw anybody more surprised. The early morning hours between two and 6 A.M. are the best time to nab criminals, anywhere.

As we questioned the suspect, I saw him glance toward his pillow and guessed he had a gun hidden under it. He suddenly dived for the pillow and almost got two revolvers into play, but we disarmed him easily and snapped on the handcuffs.

Later in the day Miss Velez and her business manager, Bo Roos, accompanied me to the butler's apartment to identify her property. His rooms were stacked with trunks and boxes and bags full of silverware, dishes, linens and other valuables—between $5,000 and $10,000 worth at today's prices. We found much more stuff than the Mexican actress had reported stolen, and she suggested checking with Mary Astor who had previously employed the butler.

Next morning I called on Miss Astor in her Spanish-style home at the corner of Benedict Canyon Drive and Tower Road and advised her of the situation. The pretty redhead took a quick inventory of her house, with the housekeeper, and discovered that the balance of the stolen goods, several thousand dollars worth, belonged to her.

Miss Astor was not aware her home had been looted. She was in the process of getting a divorce from Dr. Franklyn Thorpe and had been too preoccupied to keep an eye on her property. The situation was ripe for the dishonest butler to carry off whatever he wanted. I have noticed that domestics get smart fast in homes where divorces are pending. The servants know that neither side wants to antagonize them because of their value as witnesses, and if any property disappears from the house the husband or wife will assume the other has taken it.

A former butler led us a long chase when a $75,000 diamond-and-platinum necklace of Mrs. Doris Warner Vidor vanished. Mrs. Vidor, wife of the late motion-picture director, Charles Vidor, missed the valuable necklace after moving from Beverly Hills to Bel-Air. In the general confusion of moving, nobody was quite sure what had happened to it.

We spent weeks questioning servants, movers, cleaners, decorators and others who had been employed in the houses during the moving. None of them remembered seeing the necklace. We posted it as missing and awaited developments.

Not long afterward we got a rumble on a man named Paul Winters who had once worked as a butler for the Vidors. Winters, who also used an alias, was caught as he tried to sell the Vidor necklace along with other jewelry which had disappeared from two Bel-Air and Brentwood homes where he had worked as butler. One home was the residence of Nancy Oakes, socially prominent daughter of the millionaire, Sir Harry Oakes, who had been bludgeoned to death mysteriously in the Bahamas some years earlier.

Winters proved to have a fantastic background. He had a record of two larceny arrests by the Metropolitan Police of London, England. Later he had exchanged identifications with an American soldier who wanted to stay in England after World War II. Using the soldier's credentials and assuming his name, Winters arrived in the United States on a military transport and made his way to Beverly Hills, where his impeccable British accent helped him get a job as a butler. Few of his employers, if any, took the trouble to check carefully into his references.

Winters got away with Mrs. Vidor's necklace unseen and unsuspected. He knew that the family was moving, and was familiar with the layout of the spacious home. He also knew where the necklace was kept, and felt sure its theft would not be discovered until the Vidors unpacked in their new home. It was a simple matter for him to enter the house and remove the necklace; his mistake was in trying to sell it. He was deported back to England after serving a sentence in State prison.

On a hot Sunday afternoon in August, 1933, Norman Philp, a wealthy retired dairy-owner, opened the wall safe in his home on North Linden Drive. It had been two weeks since his previous visit to the safe. His custom was to open it only on the first and 15th of each month to get his checkbook and write the necessary checks for household expenses.

As he thumbed through the papers in the safe he suddenly became aware that a bundle of negotiable bonds, $73,000 worth, was missing. He made a careful recheck of the contents of the safe and discovered that $2000 in cash was also gone. He quickly called police headquarters, and I was assigned as detective on the case. In 1933, at the depth of the depression, $75,000 was a fantastic sum of money!

It was a puzzling case because there was no physical evidence that a crime had been committed. The safe had not been tampered with, there was no sign of entry into the house by a prowler, and other valuables were in their usual place. The two maids employed in the house knew nothing about the theft. There had been a butler, Steve Palinkas, but he had quit his job more than a month before the burglary and had moved back East. Recently he had sent the maids a postal card from Cleveland where he was now living.

We took the usual precaution of putting a stop order on the bonds and notifying the issuing companies that the securities were missing. Four months later an attorney in Cleveland called Mr. Philp by long-distance telephone to report that he had a client in his office who had bought $15,000 worth of the missing bonds in good faith. His client had tried to sell them and learned they were reported stolen. However, he would be willing to stand part of the loss if Mr. Philp would buy them back for $10,000.

This call came in on Friday night, and the lawyer made an appointment to call back on Monday to get Mr. Philp's answer. I arranged immediately to fly to Cleveland. However, it was no easy three-hour jet flight. Commercial aviation was still in its infancy and the airplane was a tri-motor Ford. It took all day Saturday and most of Sunday, with a stopover at Kansas City, to get me to the Ohio city, but I managed to arrive at the lawyer's office early Monday morning. I wanted to get a good look at his client. When I walked into the office there was Palinkas, the former butler!

I walked out of the office with both the bonds and Palinkas in my custody. I mailed the bonds to Beverly Hills and locked up the butler in the police station, with the assistance of Captain of Detectives Frank Story, who is now Cleveland's Chief of Police. I would not be able to take my prisoner back home until after extradition, but at least the bonds were recovered. That evening when I returned to my hotel two deputy sheriffs were waiting for me with a writ to attach the bonds. Palinkas had hired another attorney and was claiming ownership of the securities. I had to tell the deputies, regretfully, that they were too late.

Palinkas put up a month-long fight against extradition. He first claimed he had bought the bonds, later said his employer had given them to him, and finally asserted he had been with relatives in Ohio and Pennsylvania when the alleged crime had been committed. I visited his relatives in an attempt to locate the thousands of dollars worth of bonds still missing. I found no trace of the bonds, but in questioning his niece in Sharon, Pennsylvania, I learned that he had asked her to get affidavits from various people establishing the fact that he had been in Ohio and Pennsylvania. It was true, she said, that Palinkas had been in the East all the time, except for one short trip to California which had taken him only a few days.

This confirmed my belief that Palinkas had been in Beverly Hills when the bonds disappeared. Another officer arrived from California with extradition papers for the butler, and within a short time we returned him to Los Angeles County for trial and sentencing.

Palinkas later told us how he had taken the bonds. While vacuum-cleaning the house he had found the combination to the safe on a card hidden under a corner of the living-room rug. Knowing that his wealthy employer kept considerable cash and valuables in the safe, Palinkas had a duplicate key made for the front door and quit his job, ostensibly to move East. He sent a postcard from Cleveland to establish his presence there, then backtracked to Beverly Hills and entered the house on a Thursday night when he knew the maids would be out and the master dining elsewhere. With a key to the front door and the combination to the safe it took him only a few minutes to get the bonds and cash. He left for the East immediately, knowing that his theft would not be noticed until two weeks later when the owner opened the safe.

Our investigation of Palinkas uncovered a nationwide conspiracy to violate immigration and customs laws. We found that he was one of a group of Hungarian immigrants who had entered the United States illegally with falsified papers supplied by a New York steamship agent. The agent, who had forged passports for a number of clients, shook them down regularly for "payoff money" which he said went to government officials. He periodically demanded $200 from

112

each of his victims to ward off their deportation, a racket frequently practiced on foreign-born residents here.

Palinkas and a friend of his named Balong, who worked as a houseman in New York and Connecticut, and their wives, were all paying off. Balong, who was an escapee from a Hungarian prison, was picked up in New York City by Lieutenant Grover Brown and Detective Henry Oswald, police officers of the Main Office Squad, after they had traced him far and near. The steamship agent and several immigration officials and customs men were indicted, and the Hungarians were deported, Palinkas among them, after he served his California sentence for burglary. We worked closely with Immigration Agent Perley Dunn of Los Angeles, since retired, in this investigation.

The rest of the missing bonds were never found. Palinkas claimed he had burned them when he suspected that the police were on his trail. New bonds were issued to the owner replacing those allegedly destroyed.

A methodical German butler named Ewald Schwebs victimized a score of servants in Beverly Hills before we caught up with him. On payday nights he would walk the streets between 6 and 9 P.M., looking for houses where the servants were busy serving dinner. Wherever he saw the servants occupied he would ransack their quarters, taking only cash. This was in the days when servants were paid in cash on the first and 15th of the month and occupied separate quarters at the rear of each estate.

Schwebs would "hit" the servants' quarters and be safe at home before they discovered his thefts. On two occasions he took more than cash. At Gertrude Niesen's home he picked up a fountain pen bearing the name of the blonde singing star, and at another stop he walked off with a pair of butler's trousers.

The thefts were as regular as clockwork: Two burglary calls on the first of the month, two more calls on the 15th, and always in servants' quarters. With this in mind I picked a night and patroled the area in my own car so as not to alarm the burglar. Within a short time I spotted a man peering in the front window of a large home where a dinner party was in progress. As I watched him he quickly walked to the rear of the house. I followed, quietly, and grabbed him just as he forced open a door in the servants' quarters.

My suspect insisted he was there to call on his girl friend, but I handcuffed him and inquired among the domestics in the house. None of them knew him. I then learned he worked as a butler in the 900 block on North Roxbury Drive, approximately two miles away, and took him to his room in the rear of a large estate. Here I found Miss Niesen's pen, with her name scratched off, and the butler's trousers which had previously been reported stolen.

Schwebs admitted he had burglarized 20 servants' quarters in two months. In checking into his past I found he had formerly been a policeman in Germany and had absconded with the company funds of his police barracks. An American tourist had picked him up and brought him to this country to work as a butler. After he served a sentence in State prison, Schwebs was deported.

We once had a general housekeeper in Beverly Hills who was famous as the "perfect servant." For a time housewives vied with each other to employ this household jewel. Unfortunately, however, she developed larcenous tendencies. She would be a model employee for several weeks at each new situation, but sooner or later she would burglarize the place. She was sent to the women's prison at Tehachapi and unofficially was put on our "inactive" list.

We were surprised, a short time later, when another case identical with hers was reported. Investigation revealed that the culprit was the same "perfect servant." She had escaped from Tehachapi and the authorities there had failed to notify us. We finally located her in the State of Washington, near Seattle, and brought her back, and she was again sentenced to the women's prison.

One enterprising domestic completely furnished a five-room house, from front door to back, with expensive draperies, carpets, furniture, dishes and silverware stolen from a wealthy divorcee in Beverly Hills. The divorcee had moved from a sixteen-room house into smaller quarters and stored her leftover belongings in a double garage. She seldom had occasion to enter the garage, and didn't notice the theft until months later when she went looking for her silver serving set. It was missing, along with other property, and she called the police. We found her servant living in temporary luxury in Long Beach, 25 miles away, silver serving set and all. It required a moving van to haul the loot back to Beverly Hills.

During 30 years I have arrested a number of domestic employees of radio, television and motion-picture celebrities, but in many cases I have had to release them because of their employers' aversion to publicity. Prominent citizens frequently will refuse to prosecute dishonest servants.

I remember the mistress of a large house who was immensely proud of a thriving garden which the maid and her husband, the houseman, had planted around their living quarters at the rear of the estate. However, she had to call the police one morning when the maid went berserk in the kitchen and threw a skillet at her, causing considerable wreckage. When we arrived at the house the mistress commented sadly on her maid's unusual behavior. She couldn't understand it because the maid and houseman were such a fine couple and seemed to like the place. She pointed out the "beautiful plants" they were cultivating as she conducted us to the servants' quarters. Inside we found the maid, hopped up, and her husband smoking a marijuana cigarette. Their garden was 100 per cent marijuana plants.

Another maid at a party given by a wealthy paint manufacturer on Crescent Drive let her ex-convict boy friend into a back bedroom where he stole several thousand dollars worth of jewelry. The loss was discovered during the party, and the maid suspected, but the host asked us not to question her until the following day. He wanted nothing to interfere with the pleasure of his guests. By the next day the maid had a good alibi and solution of the theft was delayed.

115

Ten months later I got a telephone call in my office from a woman who identified herself as the maid. She stated she had news for me regarding the stolen jewelry and asked me to meet her, alone, at the corner of Fifty-first Street and Avalon Boulevard in Los Angeles. I kept the appointment, not knowing whether it was a trap or what to expect, and took the precaution of having a partner keep me under surveillance from a distance with high-power glasses. If anything unusual happened, he was to join me.

However, the maid only wanted to tell me the true story of the burglary, as she was now angry at her ex-boy friend. She said she had let him in the house and he had taken the jewelry, but afterwards he had jilted her and run away with another woman. She was now ready to testify against her former lover. Later we contacted her at home where she introduced us to her husband and their baby.

Meanwhile we apprehended the ex-boy friend and prepared to go to trial, since we now had a witness who could definitely establish the man's activity on the night of the crime. However, when we placed her on the witness stand at the trial, the defense attorney objected and asked the court's permission to examine her eligibility as a witness. To our chagrin he established that the maid was wife of the defendant, still married to him even though she was living with another man by whom she had a child. She had not bothered to get a divorce.

We were understandably surprised by this new development, and our burglary suspect went free on a technicality. However, crime did not pay for him. He sold the jewelry for counterfeit money and was picked up and imprisoned by the United States Secret Service for passing bogus money.

Some years ago José Iturbi, the famous pianist and long-time resident of Beverly Hills, befriended a young man who wanted to be a singer by giving him a job as butler in his home on Benedict Canyon Drive. This was shortly after the death of Mr. Iturbi's daughter, and he was extremely concerned for the welfare of her two children who lived with him.

116

His new butler, aware of the pianist's concern for his grandchildren, set out to make a record as a family protector. On several occasions he reported to his employer that he had seen prowlers near the house and frightened them away. Later he described to Mr. Iturbi how he had bested some more prowlers in physical combat.

Our patrol officers investigated the butler's reports but could find no trace of intruders in the vicinity. However, Mr. Iturbi naturally was alarmed and incensed at what apparently was lack of proper police protection for his home. He telephoned my office to demand that something be done about the plague of prowlers in his neighborhood. I went to the pianist's house to investigate and to interview the butler. I became convinced the man was not telling the truth and challenged his stories. Finally he admitted they were hoaxes. He said he was only trying to gain the admiration of Mr. Iturbi, who had befriended him. He just wanted to make himself invaluable! I reminded him he would not be valuable to Mr. Iturbi in jail and departed. As far as I know he never saw another prowler.

twelve

BURGLARS

IN THE HILLS

IN THEIR OWN WARPED WAY, BURGLARS LIKE BEVERLY
Hills almost as much as tourists do—maybe more. The
lovely, secluded canyons winding up into the Santa Monica
Mountains, the millionaires' estates, the tall palms and other
beautiful trees and shrubbery which charm honest visitors to
our city, unfortunately stir only larceny in the hearts of
second-story men. Large and expensive homes on tree-shaded
streets, with plenty of shrubbery for concealment, are a challenge to this criminal brotherhood.

Since the temptations here are so great, we take extraor-
dinary measures to keep thieves away, such as maintaining
24-hour vigilance with our police radio patrol cars. In a
normal year we nab about 50 burglars, and make life considerably more hazardous for the few persistent fellows who
succeed in sneaking past us. Take Greta Garbo's prowler, for
instance.

Miss Garbo, who was a Beverly Hills resident for many
years, was awakened late one night by the sound of foot-

steps in her home on North Bedford Drive. The actress, who, as all the world knows, prefers to live alone, made a swift and dramatic exit from an upstairs window, clad only in her nightgown. She scrambled down a drainpipe and ran next door to spread the alarm. Shortly afterwards a dim figure sprinted from her house, climbed a fence, fled across a neighboring back yard and disappeared.

When police arrived, Miss Garbo was gathering up loot which had been thrown away by the panic-stricken thief in his hasty flight. She found her red coin purse with $55 in it, a small clock, and some food ration tickets, which were valuable in 1944 when this happened. Two coats, one of them mink, had been tossed into a hedge beside her house.

Miss Garbo was never bothered by burglars again, but other movie homes here have been "hit" by prowlers from time to time. I remember one ingenious thief who was captured in the stately white Georgian home of Jack L. Warner in broad daylight, when the head of Warner Brothers studios was entertaining Hollywood celebrities at a Sunday afternoon tennis party on his estate. The prowler, dressed in natty tennis shorts and carrying a racquet, was seen by an alert maid as he entered the master bedroom. He was in the right costume, but the wrong room. The maid knew that all the guests were supposed to be at the tennis courts and pool, where a snack bar had been set up. She called the guard at the gate, who summoned police. Our patrol cars converged on the house from front and rear within a few minutes, but it took us half an hour of searching, through many rooms and closets, before we cornered the culprit.

We had another burglar who always worked during the early evening hours and majored in large homes, including those of Bing Crosby, Victor Fleming, Reginald Owens and Barney Padway.

In the 1930s, the homes of Barbara Stanwyck, Richard Barthelmess and other screen celebrities were broken into by a gang of burglars which systematically picked up furs, jewels and valuables worth $250,000, and disposed of them through "fences" in San Francisco, Portland, Spokane, and Yakima, Washington. Alert police work rounded up the burglars, as well as their confederates in the Northwest.

The top member of this crew was their second-story man, the Cat Burglar, who was sentenced to San Quentin Prison for a long term. He was a model prisoner at first, and smart enough to get a responsible job as chief clerk to Warden Clinton Duffy. His job enabled him to move around the prison freely and eventually to make his escape, after which he returned to Beverly Hills and burglary.

The first time we caught him he had parked his car on a Beverly Hills street after midnight, near a house he was robbing. Patrol officers, who view with suspicion any automobile left on our streets after hours, stopped to investigate his car and picked him up when he returned to it with an armload of loot, thus earning himself another stretch at San Quentin.

The Cat Burglar, a persistent type, did not make the same mistake twice. On his next foray, some years later, he parked outside the city limits and crept into an exclusive residential district between 2 and 5 A.M., hiding in hedges and shrubbery near houses whenever a patrol car passed.

Cat Man, slippery as quicksilver, was aptly named. Quick as a rabbit and fearless, he would take off his shoes and steal into bedrooms where people were sleeping, lift wallets out of pockets and noiselessly take jewelry off dressers.

In spite of his skill, however, he spent much of his time behind bars. When I last heard of him he was 41 years of age and had served nine prison terms in three States, Minnesota, Oregon and California. I am sure other police officers in California join me in hoping he has taken up some other line of work.

The best burglar I ever met was the Pet Editor, a fellow who wrote articles on the care and feeding of pets as a sideline to his pilfering. He was a repeat offender who had picked up his knowledge of animals by studying in prison. Many prisoners, with nothing to do for five or 10 years, take up

120

hobbies and become phenomenal experts in their fields. The Birdman of Alcatraz is a good example of a prisoner who became an authority.

The Pet Editor had more brass than most burglars. He would choose houses at random, walk into them in daylight, steal whatever he wanted. Once we caught him walking down a Beverly Hills street discarding stolen jewelry, piece by piece, which he had decided was worthless. We made him retrace his steps and recovered several thousand dollars worth of gems which he had tossed into a vacant lot and a hedge.

I first met the Pet Editor one summer afternoon as I was driving along a residential street which was largely deserted because the homeowners were away on vacation. I saw two fellows standing on the sidewalk, and my curiosity was aroused when one of them walked up a driveway toward a large house, while his partner looked up and down the street.

I wheeled my Chevrolet touring car around in the middle of the block and went back to check the man on the sidewalk. He took me into his confidence readily, though with some show of embarrassment. It was a rather delicate matter, he said. He and his pal had met a couple of married women at a dance and were about to call on their new friends at home, but first they wanted to make sure that no husbands were in the immediate vicinity.

His story seemed reasonable enough, and I was just about to believe it when I heard the sound of glass shattering on the porch. A voice called out from the house: "It's okay, Joe. I've got the door open!" With that I snapped handcuffs on my fast talking friend, linking him to the steering wheel of my patrol car, hurried into the house and collared his confederate, who turned out to be the Pet Editor.

This was before the days of radio communication when it was more difficult to call headquarters for help and there were fewer officers available to render aid. There was nothing else for me to do but to handcuff my suspects together in a manner which would make it difficult for them to escape, and I kept one hand on my nightstick in case this pair tried any backseat driving. It wasn't the first time nor the last that I've felt like a Keystone cop.

A young and handsome rare-book expert, The Doctor, engineered robberies of several wealthy Beverly Hills women interested in rare books. We became aware of his activities when investigation of three house entries revealed that all the victims were friends of the bookman. One woman remembered that the robber wanted certain first editions which only one familiar with her house would know.

A veteran Beverly Hills officer broke up The Doctor's little scheme by posing as a hardened ex-convict from Canon City, Colorado, and joining his gang of six thieves, who were all sharing living quarters with their leader. Here the detective bumped into the most fantastic story he had ever heard.

The gang was planning to raise $600,000 by a series of burglaries and robberies. They needed the money to finance an armed aerial expedition to Mexico where they would hijack a ton of gold from the Yaqui Indians of Southern Sonora. The Doctor, who, at the time, was a son-in-law of one of the wealthiest Americans in Mexico, claimed to know where the gold was, and would lead them to it. The gang was to land in a transport plane bristling with guns, fight off the fierce Yaquis with cannon and grenades, load the gold aboard and smuggle it by air into the United States. They figured they could sell it for a cool $1,800,000, which would mean a nice profit all around.

After we arrested The Doctor, a literary type, he claimed the whole thing was just a plot for a novel he was writing. However, there was nothing fictional about the $20,000 his accomplices had netted, and Doc was sent to prison. While there he spent his time delving into various religious philosophies and eventually became an authority. After his release he bought a degree for $200 from a local diploma mill which dubbed him "Doctor of Religious Science."

The last time I heard from him he had just given a lec-

Back in 1919 when the movie stars began building showplace homes in the foothills west of Hollywood, Douglas Fairbanks, Senior, shown here attending a premiere with his wife, Mary Pickford, suggested putting a wall around our little six-square-mile city to keep it exclusive. The wall never materialized, but an invisible economic wall nevertheless set Beverly Hills apart.

The Duke and Duchess of Windsor almost got a traffic ticket a few minutes after this picture was taken outside the Beverly Hills Hotel, but luckily I was able to prevent a diplomatic "incident."

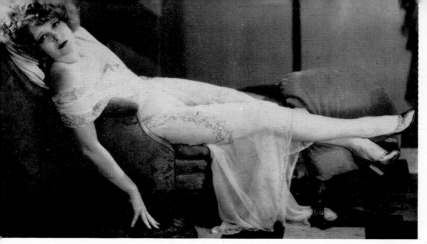

I remember Clara Bow's frightened brown eyes peering through the peephole in her front door as I removed an unwelcome visitor from the premises. All he wanted to do was marry her!

Will Rogers was our most popular citizen during my patrolman days. The whole town turned out to welcome him as honorary Mayor in 1926 at a ceremony in the park across the street from the Beverly Hills Hotel. Conrad Nagel is behind him, and Mrs. Rogers and the children at the right of the platform.

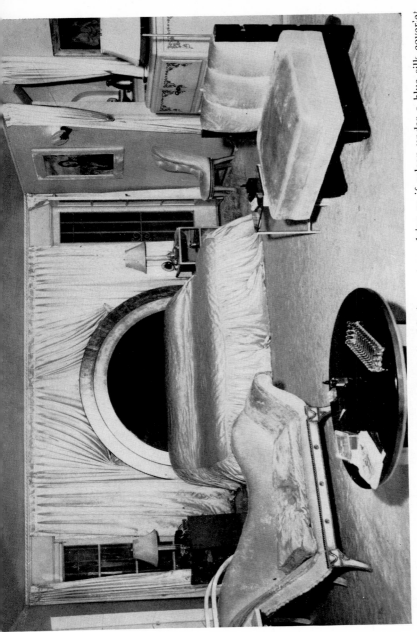

We found Lupe Velez, the beautiful and tempestuous Mexican actress, lying as if asleep under a blue silk coverlet in this ornate bedroom, dead by her own hand. She left a suicide note addressed to her faithless lover by the telephone beside her bed.

The Chaplin-Berry paternity case was probably the lengthiest litigation of its kind in local history. Here is the dramatic highlight of the trial as the controversial little comedian strikes a somber pose along with Joan Berry and her baby, Carol Ann, in front of the jury box.

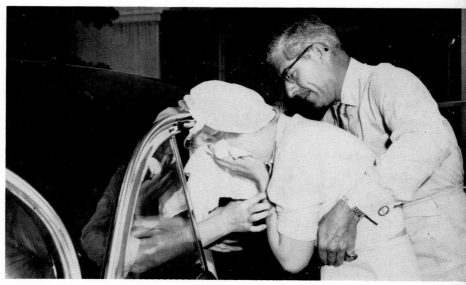

Actress Marie MacDonald, once famous as "The Body," staged a one-woman riot in our jail when we arrested her after an automobile collision in 1954. She cut a wide swathe through newspaper photographers when we released her. Later she charged us with brutality!

Tragedy was only a few days away when this smiling trio posed at Los Angeles International Airport: Lana Turner, Johnny Stompanato, and her daughter, Cheryl Crane. We had already been advised that Miss Turner had been threatened by her handsome escort.

Careful comparison of the fingerprints on the murder weapon with those of Cheryl Crane established the truth of the girl's story.

Everybody except the police department was shocked when Al Teitelbaum, famous movie furrier, was convicted for staging a fake fur robbery at his store. Some of Hollywood's biggest "names" were his character witnesses, but he went to jail—after three years of legal maneuvering.

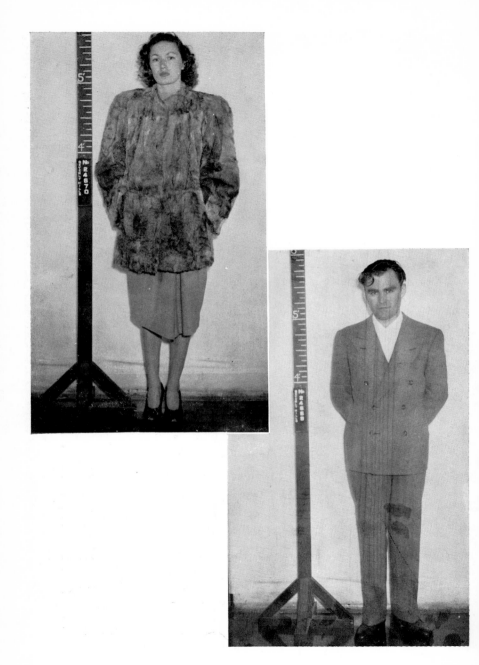

WESTERN UNION

1213

A. N. WILLIAMS
PRESIDENT

NEWCOMB CARLTON
CHAIRMAN OF THE BOARD

J. C. WILLEVER
FIRST VICE-PRESIDENT

Send the following telegram, subject to the terms on back hereof, which are hereby agreed to

To _____ . 19___

Street and No. THIS CHECQUE HANDED YOU — REPRESENTS $3,000 CURRon Place To BE GIVEN To ME by YOU. — IN SMALL CURANCY $100.00 $50.00 AND $20.00

THIS CHILD IN MY ARMS IS NOT MY OWN, IT LIVES IN THE NEIGHbORHOOD, AND iTS LIFE DEPENDS SOLEY ON YOUR WILLINGNESS To DO AS TOLD.

REFRAIN FROM GIVING AN ALARM OR TRYING TO SIGNAL IN ANY FORM! YOU WILL bE KILLED FIRST — THEN THE CHILD.

THESE ARE YOUR INSTRUCTIONS

WANT A REPLY? "Answer by WESTERN UNION" or similar phrases may be included without charge.

Sender's address for reference

Sender's telephone number

WESTERN UNION

1213

A. N. WILLIAMS
PRESIDENT

NEWCOMB CARLTON
CHAIRMAN OF THE BOARD

J. C. WILLEVER
FIRST VICE-PRESIDENT

Send the following telegram, subject to the terms on back hereof, which are hereby agreed to

To _____ . 19___

Street and No. I WANT PACKAGED MONEY THAT DOes NOT REQUIRE COUNTING — ONE QUIVER OF YOUR LIPS AND iT WILL bE YOUR LAST WARNING

(1) IF POSSIbLE CALL FOR THE MONEY (IF NOT)
(2) GET THE MONEY — STAY IN SIGHT

ADDRESS NO ONE, ACT NATURAL

RETURN HERE WITH THE CASH

SIT DOWN — REMAIN QUIET AND NO ALARM FOR FIVE MINUTES, UNLESS YOU WANT THE DEATH OF THIS CHILD! THIS IS INSURED MONEY — SO DONT BE A HERO — UNLESS YOUR LIFE IS ONLY VALUED AT $3,000 I HAVE THE BEAD ON YOU AS YOU READ THIS!

WANT A REPLY? "Answer by WESTERN UNION" or similar phrases may be included without charge.

Sender's address for reference

Sender's telephone number

Two visitors with a borrowed baby and these hold-up notes took a Beverly Hills bank for $1200, but we nabbed them in 24 hours.

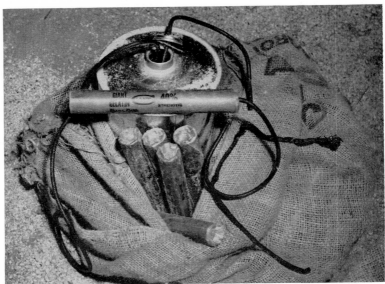

Charley, the "mad bomber," (center) fainted dead away in police headquarters when we caught him trying to blow up seven homes in Beverly Hills and Los Angeles with home-made time bombs. One of Charley's bombs, a soft-drink syrup can stuffed with dynamite sticks, was found with the fuse sputtering under a doctor's window in our city. An alert patrolman stamped out the fuse.

We found a fortune in stolen jewelry when we broke into the Beverly Hills hideout of Gerard Graham Dennis, the international "Raffles." He had collected rubies, emeralds, and diamonds larger than dimes.

Dennis, probably the most efficient and daring jewel thief of his time, on his way to prison for a 18-year-to-life stay. He had several weaknesses, notably his own ego and the girls.

Bugsy Siegel had a gold key to the front door of this handsome Beverly Hills home rented by his red-headed friend, Virginia Hill. He was reading a newspaper in the living-room when a gangland assassin, hidden outside a window, got him on June 20, 1947. What a place to die!

Bugsy Siegel's killing was a perfectly staged gangland execution and is still on our unsolved list. The grisly assassination ended Bugsy's activities in top Hollywood society where he had been sponsored by the fabulous, fun-loving Countess di Frasso.

A few minutes after he took two potshots at a Hollywood agent, Walter Wanger posed for this "mug shot" in our jail. In view of the mild treatment he received for a serious offense, we were greatly surprised at the nature and slanting of his next motion picture.

Walter Wanger's arrest brought some top legal talent to my office. That's Jerry Giesler, defense lawyer, with his hand on Wanger's shoulder, and (at left) the then District Attorney of Los Angeles County, the late Ernest Roll.

We never had much trouble with Tony Cornero in Beverly Hills, but he led officers a merry chase as "admiral" of an offshore gambling fleet in 1939. He died gambling.

Elmer Perry, a professional gambler with a police record, was considered a public benefactor by some citizens, but his social club, frequented by civic and fraternal groups, was a front for big-time gambling. He died in a gangland slaying.

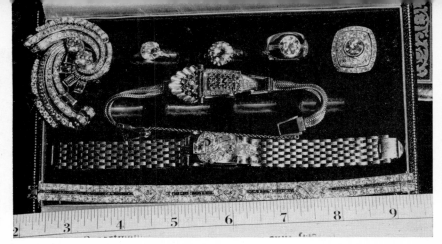

We arrested a confidence man after he claimed he "lost" these valuable baubles which had been left with him for sale. He told a thrilling story of being kidnapped and robbed, but we found the jewelry buried in a can in his father-in-law's back yard.

This was the haul of just one female shoplifter! We had a trio of them who stocked a store in a neighboring city with thousands of dollars worth of stolen goods which they sold as "reclaimed merchandise."

These swift Harley-Davidson motorcycles are a far cry from the bicycles we pedalled in my early days.

Police officers such as these fine men and women shown in front of the Beverly Hills City Hall devote their lives to law enforcement. In spite of drudgery, low pay, slow advancement, legal harassments and what sometimes seems to be apathy on the part of the public, police work has a powerful appeal for them because they are protecting society, serving their community and upholding the law. If necessary they are willing to make the supreme sacrifice.

ture at a local university, and was trying to contact lonely, wealthy women interested in religious and philosophical instruction. I invited him to my office and warned him that much as I valued the higher things of life my department would keep a strict scrutiny on his relationship with his feminine clients. He flashed his doctor's degree on me, but I reminded him that although he could buy a phony Ph.D., the institution he had really graduated from—we call it San Quentin in California—was not the degree granting type.

A hillbilly from Arkansas had an efficient little burglary operation going before we caught up with him. He only stole stuff for which he had "orders." He would station himself at a transcontinental truck depot in Los Angeles and ask the various drivers what items they would like to buy to take home with them—typewriters, tires, dresses, anything. With orders at hand, he would set forth to assemble the goods.

He worked only on Sundays and preferred Beverly Hills. One Sunday evening on patrol I saw a man at a bus stop hide a tennis racquet behind his back as I drove past. This seemed rather peculiar, so I stopped and asked him if he was a tennis player and where had he been playing. All tennis court lights had been turned off for the night by this time. He didn't have a satisfactory answer. I found the owner's name and address on the racquet and took my suspect to the house. Here we discovered he had also taken cash. Further questioning of the man cleared up several burglaries of miscellaneous articles—typewriters, wearing apparel and sport equipment—and ended the illegal mercantile career of our Arkansas visitor.

I don't know if there is an affinity between burglars and Communists, but the fact is that we have arrested several thieves who were bright pink politically.

One of them was a 28-year-old writer we caught burglarizing office buildings on week-ends. He was an Eastern newspaper man who had tried to make a living in Hollywood writing movie and television scripts, but had finally resorted to bad checks and burglary.

When he was apprehended leaving an office building late on a Sunday night he claimed to be an elevator inspector and showed, as proof, an elevator operator's manual in his brief case. However, the arresting officer took him back inside the building and found two offices had been broken into. He also discovered a large supply of stamps and cash on the suspect, who admitted he had been prowling buildings in the vicinity of his apartment.

In his apartment we found manuscripts criticizing the police and their treatment of criminals, which the prisoner said he had written at the request of a Los Angeles County probation officer, since dismissed, who had befriended him while he was in jail for passing bad checks. The probation officer had taken him home as a house guest, after his release, and shown him confidential files concerning prominent people who had been arrested and asked him to write Communist-slanted articles for scandal magazines.

At the officer's request he had also launched a "Letters to the Editor" campaign in local newspapers, attacking judges, police and law enforcement methods. He kept the campaign going by writing derogatory answers to his own letters under various names. Thus, what appeared to be a hot debate in a public forum was really only a one-man smoke screen.

The probation officer was discharged after these facts were revealed, but not before some of his propaganda had got into print.

The Red Raider of Beverly Hills was a clever, well-informed Communist who knew every corner of the party organization in California, and used this information to keep out of the penitentiary. He looked like an intellectual, a scholar in horn-rimmed eyeglasses, but he was an inveterate burglar who led police a chase for several years. He acquired his nickname by boasting that he burglarized the homes of the rich only to raise money for Communist causes.

He was an ex-convict who had served time in San Quentin, where he struck up a friendship with Tom Mooney, the San Francisco dynamiter, who became the martyred saint of California radicals before his death. (The Red Raider was carrying a letter of recommendation from Mooney when we arrested him.) After leaving prison, he had worked on the San Francisco waterfront for the Communists, was secretary of the northern branch of the party, and membership director.

In 1937, when he was caught in a burglary, the Red Raider blew the whistle on every top Communist on the West Coast. He became a star witness for the Dies Committee on Un-American Activities in Washington, D.C., and linked the names of Harry Bridges and several political and labor leaders with Communist activities.

Sentenced to Folsom Prison for burglary, he begged the court's leniency on the ground that to send him to State Prison would mean his certain death at the hands of his former Communist pals. His plea impressed a United States Senator, who interceded for him. Governor Frank Merriam of California ordered him released from custody as a reward for his services to the Federal government.

Eighteen months later we arrested the Red Raider for burglary in Beverly Hills. He was caught with $20,000 worth of plunder he had taken from a home. He had run from the scene of the crime, but thoughtlessly had left his automobile standing in front of the looted house. This time, he told us, he was raising money to contribute to causes *opposed* to Communism! Faced with a State Prison sentence as an habitual offender, he again avoided it by informing on Red activities and served his time in the County Jail instead.

Ten years later the Red Raider was back in jail for a burglarly in San Marino, California. He had been shot and seriously wounded as he tried to run away from the scene of the crime. And, for a third time, his record as a Communist informer saved him from the penitentiary and allowed him to do his time in County Jail.

I learned a little bit about Communist techniques myself from the Red Raider. When we first arrested him he implicated a labor organizer in a burglary, and made an appointment to meet the man in a Los Angeles hotel. I followed him to the rendezvous, and grabbed his partner in the hotel lobby. Later the partner complained I had pinioned his arms so suddenly he did not have time to follow the party line. When I inquired what the line called for at the time of an arrest, he explained that Communists are instructed to yell and put up resistance in order to draw a crowd, and in the confusion to escape. Since detectives wear plain clothes an arrest can be made to look like a struggle between two men, one of whom is in need of help.

We recently caught a 20-year-old church burglar, who had looted a local rectory on successive Sunday nights, and found him to be an expert in at least one phase of religious activity. He knew when offerings were taken and where the collection money was kept in churches of all denominations, Protestant, Catholic and Jewish, in many parts of the United States.

He admitted to 400 church burglaries. It took us a month of steady correspondence with other police departments to clear up his other burglaries, and he finally was sent to State Prison. Before we caught up with him he had lived lavishly on his church loot, spending it in nightclubs where he was known as a heavy tipper by waiters and entertainers.

The all-time record for single-handed thievery in this vicinity is still held by a retired gentleman burglar, who has been residing for some years now in a New York State prison. Gerard Graham Dennis, the Canadian "Raffles," acquired illegally more than $600,000 worth of jewels and furs in Beverly Hills, Bel-Air, and the wealthy suburbs of Westchester County, New York, before detectives ended his transcontinental burglary spree in 1949.

He was an escaped convict from Canada when he slipped into Beverly Hills after pulling a series of burglaries in New York State. Sleek-haired, blue-eyed, 28-year-old Dennis posed as a wealthy playboy actor and jewel salesman, and used snob tactics on his prospective victims. He lived in a swank apartment on Oakhurst Drive, mingled with motion-picture and society celebrities, and followed newspaper society pages closely for information.

When a glittering party drew scores of guests, bedecked with furs, jewels and valuables, Dennis was on hand in his tailored tuxedo, walking in the front door along with the other guests.

His operation was highly efficient. He drew maps of the houses he entered, made notes on the size of the family, description and age of each member, and probable wealth in jewels. When he was thoroughly familiar with the layout of a house, he would return in mask and gloves, carrying a gun, and break in and steal. A muscular and agile man, he climbed drainpipes to second stories when necessary.

He rarely bothered with houses that cost less than $100,000. His theory was that any husband who could afford such luxury would also have his wife loaded with jewels. Dennis took one Bel-Air home for $257,000 worth of jewels, bracelets and necklaces, his prize haul locally. He also made off with $32,000 worth of furs and jewels belonging to Loretta Young, stole jewels valued at $15,000 from Mrs. Mack Gordon, widow of the songwriter, and lifted another $15,000 in gems from Mrs. Dolly Walker, daughter of one of the founders of Beverly Hills.

He was reported to be "polite" and "a perfect gentleman" by a woman who encountered him by surprise while he was ransacking her home. She was seated in her den reading, when Dennis suddenly entered the room looking for valuables. She told police he sat down and talked to her for five or ten minutes, real friendly like, before walking off with her jewels.

Dennis was probably the greatest jewel thief of his time, but like many other criminals he had a terrific ego that finally caught up with him. He got careless about girls and pawn shops. The end came when he gave a pretty 22-year-old model in New York City some "hot" diamond earrings to sell for him on commission. Police spotted the stolen jewelry and picked up the girl, who led them to his New York apartment where they found recent photographs of him.

His picture was circulated widely in a police bulletin, one copy of which a Cleveland, Ohio, detective took along on a fishing trip. The detective's fishing partner, a Cleveland salesman, saw the picture and recognized Dennis as a jewelry salesman he knew as "Jerry McCabe." He passed this information along to his friend, and as a result New York and Cleveland police were waiting for Dennis when he walked into a jewelry store in the Ohio city with $20,000 worth of gems in his pocket to sell.

Police also found on Dennis at the time of his arrest his Beverly Hills address book and notified me by telephone. We went to the address on Oakhurst Drive and discovered a pretty Canadian schoolteacher living in his apartment as "Mrs. Jerry McKay." She was astounded to learn of Dennis's activities. She showed us a locked closet where he kept his things, which she had no key to open. The door was reinforced and bolted with double locks. We had to tear it down to get inside.

Inside the closet, in a locked trunk, we found Dennis's treasure trove, a glittering pile of 200 diamonds, emeralds and rubies easily worth $100,000. The stones had been removed from their settings, and near by were the melted gold and platinum pieces which had held them. There was also a complete jeweler's outfit, including scales, which the jewel thief had used in his work. Hanging above the trunk were seven fur coats worth $20,000 which had been stolen from homes in this vicinity.

Since Dennis had made the mistake of shooting and wounding a man during a burglary in New Rochelle, New York, he was put on trial in White Plains, and sentenced to 18 years to life. He made one last desperate attempt for freedom. He broke and ran when he was being escorted between the courthouse and the jail, but a rookie policeman caught him after a three-block chase. In police parlance, Dennis

128

"had some rabbit in him," meaning that a prisoner who has once escaped by running will try it again.

Twenty-two citizens of Beverly Hills, Bel-Air and Hollywood breathed easier with Dennis put away. When he was arrested he was carrying a hand-written prospect list of famous names whom he considered good for jewel looting. Among the 22 names were Charles Chapin, Ronald Colman, Alice Faye, Hedy Lamarr, Jack Benny, Dorothy Lamour, Mary Pickford, Louis B. Mayer, Lady Thelma Furness, E. L. Cord, Mrs. Henry Kaiser, Jr., and Mrs. Philip Wrigley.

Through the years, burglars have been an interesting study for me. We have had all kinds in Beverly Hills, from sneak thieves to professionals. Contrary to what the public thinks, some of them have been gifted, well-educated men. Many of them are as persistent as the itch. After capture and prison, they travel around from city to city, returning to "hit" their old haunts again if they think the detective who originally arrested them is no longer around because of transfer or retirement. I have known several of them who operated in and out of State prisons for as long as 25 years. For protection against the old-line professional burglar it is best to keep a core of veteran officers in a police department who know all the dodges and the *modus operandi* of the breed.

There are egomaniacs among burglars. One man held for us by San Francisco police admitted every burglary charged to him although he had been nowhere near the scene of some of them. He did not mind confessing; he just wanted to be known as the greatest burglar of all time. Another kept a little black book with dates and places of all his burglaries. When we arrested him his book solved a whole series of past jobs.

Honest citizens should remember that burglars, such as our man Dennis, are always on the alert for prospects. They read newspaper society pages, wedding and funeral announcements, in order to know when prominent families will be absent from home. They have been known to arrive at houses with moving vans and carry off the furniture. (In Beverly Hills we guard against this by requiring special visible licenses on moving vans.) They also frequently "hit" a house in the guise of gardeners or repair men, carrying off loot in their trucks.

A lavish display of jewelry in night clubs and restaurants is an invitation to burglary. I know of several citizens who have been trailed home from resorts outside of California by burglars who admired their jewelry. Careless talk in bars and cafes can tip off a burglar as to household habits and the maid's night out. We have had cases where "party girls" passed along information to prowlers as to what wives were out of town and what houses left unprotected by wayward husbands. There were also a larcenous madam and her boy friend, both from another city, who followed golf tournaments and frequented expensive cafes, eavesdropping on conversations of prospects, getting their auto license numbers, or trailing them home.

The best advice for anyone who has valuables worth stealing is the wartime slogan, "Watch your conversation."

And what should you, as a private citizen, do if you wake up some night to find a burglar in the house? Unless you can get away from the immediate vicinity of the prowler as rapidly as Miss Garbo and summon help, your best chance is to stay quietly where you are and call the police as soon as you can safely do so.

thirteen

UNWELCOME

VISITORS

CRIMINALS, LIKE BIRDS, HEAD SOUTH FOR THE WINTER, following "the money" to Florida and Southern California. Thus, among the select clientele of tourists attracted here by our luxury hotels, celebrities and social action, we frequently find a few choice underworld characters.

I've probably interrogated more big-shot mobsters than any other small city Chief of Police in America. Among those we have locked up during the years have been members of the old Capone gang, associates of Louis (Lepke) Buchalter in Murder, Inc., offshoots of the Detroit Purple Gang, and other eastern and midwestern mobs.

Sometimes we find they have stopped here for innocent merriment on their way to Las Vegas. We usually suggest they would be happier if they left our community, since they will be under constant scrutiny by the police if they stay. Our city ordinance requiring all ex-convicts to register with the police department is also used to discourage them.

Some ex-mobsters have settled in Beverly Hills in an

attempt to gain respectability, and the police keep an eye on them to test their sincerity. One former Cleveland gangster, who became a successful business man there in spite of his long police record, moved his family here permanently and visits them as often as his eastern business permits. When I asked him why he went to such lengths to establish a home in our city he replied that his reputation was well known in the East, and he wanted his children to be free of the stigma of his early days. In Beverly Hills, he said, they would have a better opportunity and be more secure.

I had an amusing experience with an individual who settled here several years ago after he had been listed by the California Crime Commission as an "undesirable." He had been an attorney for gangland figures in the East, and had invoked the Fifth Amendment more than 80 times before the Senate Rackets Committee in Washington, D.C., when questioned about his possible connections with gangsters. I called him to my office for an interview, to find out why he had chosen to live in this particular six-square-mile segment of the United States, when so much living-space is available elsewhere. He replied that he felt the police protection here was excellent and freed him from worrying about some of his former associates! I suggested that other communities also had good police departments, and he might enjoy life more in a larger city where he would not be noticed.

The next morning a fiery little woman, weighing about 100 pounds, came into my office, pounded on the desk, and launched a five-minute tirade at me before I could open my mouth. When she finally stopped for breath, I told her to sit down and listen for a change. "I'm not at all impressed that a man who was a lawyer for Al Capone and the labor unions, who defied the United States Senate, has to send his wife in to protect him. If your husband has a real grievance, let him come here in person and submit the facts."

He had complained to the City Council that the Chief of Police was harassing him. It struck me as ridiculous that a gangster's lawyer should grumble because police were too strict for him. Our police patrol cars still pay regular visits to his street and his house is under scrutiny at all times.

Some years ago an undesirable gambler sulked in a luxurious home here after he had been run out of Nevada by his former pals, who resented his attempt to take over Bugsy Siegel's enterprises following the latter's murder. Our radio patrol cars really made him uncomfortable. They set up road blocks at either end of his street and questioned visitors to his house. His socially-minded wife found this terribly embarrassing, and eventually the gambler moved.

A study of the habits of vice lords shows that many of them across the United States live in exclusive suburbs. Often gangsters and gamblers move into a well-policed town for protection from their associates. Because of the wealth and prominence of several ex-mobsters who have settled here, Beverly Hills gets an undue amount of publicity whenever their names are in the news. One resident was mentioned in connection with the revolt in Cuba, and others were named in Congressional hearings, but as long as they obey the law there is nothing the police can do with them. They own large homes, pay heavy taxes, and live quietly in our city. And they are fully aware of our constant surveillance.

When one gangster rented a large home in an exclusive area for three months, we kept the house under close watch and were amazed at the cross-section of visitors he had. Business men, politicians and underworld characters from all over the United States and Canada were among his callers.

I remember picking up a suspicious-looking individual in a hotel who had more than $10,000 in currency in his pockets, and not a single mark of identification on him. The labels had been removed from all his clothing, and laundry marks obliterated. There was not a name on him anywhere. We held him for 24 hours, and then released him after fingerprinting. Later we found he was a member of a New York gang, here on a vacation trip.

Another time I interrogated a former Capone associate who informed me, when I asked his occupation, that he was a Chicago "sewer cover inspector." I thought it was a gag, but the fellow went on to explain the details of his high-paying job. It seemed that whenever a loose sewer cover rattled in a Chicago street, disturbing the peace of the neighborhood and passing motorists, it was his responsibility to see that the cover was replaced with a new one that fit.

The task of removing undesirables from the vicinity is enormous and vexing. Frequently, when police arrest underworld characters with money, they find themselves on trial instead of the mobsters, because of the legal talent involved. In police terminology, we have a "make sheet", or record, on all known gangsters, and we find many of them have been arrested often and acquitted, or else the charges against them have been dismissed. The reason usually is that the mobsters can hire high-priced attorneys, well versed in legal technicalities, to cry out for their "constitutional rights." Police officers facing this kind of competition find it increasingly difficult to protect the public.

Police everywhere encounter surprising obstacles in dealing with such questionable characters. Most of them are big spenders who give lavish tips to bellboys and waitresses to insure their loyalty. Some of the best known live luxuriously at the best hotels and country clubs. They live for the present, drive expensive cars, and wear the best clothing money can buy, yet they spend much of their time and their ill-gotten gains in attempting to stay out of jail. If they devoted half as much effort to any legitimate activity, they could be successful citizens and enjoy a clear conscience.

The indignation of some unwelcome visitors we interrogate is astonishing, but seldom honest. I remember one fellow in particular who registered at an exclusive hotel with a group of New York and Miami gamblers and bookmakers. When we questioned him he was so outraged he almost turned purple. He identified himself wrathfully as an important banker from Long Island, here on vacation with influential friends, and any interference with his life, liberty and pursuit of happiness would result in the direst of consequences for the Beverly Hills Police Department. The party decided to hurry along to Las Vegas after our questioning, and we discovered a short time later that our indignant capitalist had been indicted for embezzling bank funds. I often wonder if it was the bank's money he was spending on this trip to the Nevada gambling spa.

Many mobsters follow horse-racing and often are found here during the season at Santa Anita and Hollywood Park. One visitor I recall had the worst case of racing fever I ever encountered. He was a New York attorney, who represented Frank Costello, Meyer Lansky and similar clients, and he lived for racing. At one time he had his own stable of horses. He first came to our attention when he ran up a tremendous bill at a local hotel and tried to pay it with checks that bounced. He owed the hotel some $2000, including daily rental of a limousine to take him to and from the racetrack. When we called on him at 8 A.M. he was in pajamas and bathrobe, and glassy-eyed from studying racing forms all night. Five ashtrays full of cigarette stubs, four pots of coffee, and open volumes of the *Racing Form* littered his room.

Under questioning he admitted he was broke and estimated that his racing losses totaled over $1,000,000, but he knew his fortunes would turn if he could just have a good day at the track. To avoid arrest, he persuaded hotel officials not to file charges for defaulting on an innkeeper, stating that he could easily raise the money in New York to pay his indebtedness, but when he returned to his home he was grabbed by the Bureau of Internal Revenue for failure to pay income taxes. Before the racing bug bit him he had been a successful lawyer.

Beverly Hills has residents of the sporting type who frequent Las Vegas and Monte Carlo, but these same people will not tolerate gambling in their home town. One ambitious out-of-town gambler discovered this to his sorrow when he moved his equipment into a large mansion which had formerly been occupied by two motion-picture celebrities. Certain that he would be welcomed by his former patrons, the gambler sent out invitations to them and sat back to wait for business. However, one citizen on the list felt that such an establishment did not belong in our city and notified police.

We watched the house for a week, but were puzzled by the lack of activity. It was a large place with a 200-foot frontage on Sunset Boulevard and a driveway circling the house, which was hidden behind a high hedge. Since we could see only two or three cars parked in the driveway each night, we doubted the gambling report. Two other detectives and I decided to investigate more closely, and hired a limousine in which we arrived at the front door of the mansion. As we stepped out of the car, a man dressed in a butler's uniform met us, took the automobile, and parked it out of sight in an eight-car garage behind the house. There were half a dozen other cars ahead of us, which explained the shortage of parked cars in front of the place. Looking like potential customers, we walked up a wide stairway and entered a large and ornate bedroom on the second floor. Nobody was asleep in the room. Instead, a busy crap game was going with five players in prayerful positions, and a large sum of money showing in the center. Their dismay when they saw us was intense. In another bedroom we found a "birdcage" and a card game going full blast. We picked up the gamblers and closed this infant Sunset Boulevard enterprise permanently.

Many fugitives from justice have been arrested here, and will continue to be. In handling this problem we work closely with all law enforcement agencies, local, State and Federal. Frequently when criminals commit successful crimes elsewhere they head for our local "Gold Coast." We've picked up bank robbers with their pockets filled with money, and professional criminals who come here to plot major "jobs." Because of the high "take" in their activities they can afford to spend time and money in preparation. We caught one gang of robbers from the East and South who stayed here for weeks plotting a $100,000 jewel robbery. Contrary to the movies and fiction, criminals of this stripe do not hide out in waterfront dives and garrets; they stay in the best hotels.

136

The mobster mind fascinates me. All of them, as they get older, dread their past and many try to erase the memories of it by making donations to charitable causes in an attempt to buy respectability. Some men who have been ruthless criminals in their youth later become philanthropists. No matter how big and tough they are, they are all subject to human emotions, and in time their conscience catches up with them. Yet no matter how "respectable" they become they live in fear that someone will point the finger at them. I remember Abner (Longy) Zwillman among the visitors we used to see here, at a time when the FBI labeled him "leader of the New Jersey underworld." He was a prohibition era mobster who bullied his way to gangland leadership and retired behind a façade of respectability with his ill-gotten millions. He seemed to have everything: money, influential friends and powerful political connections, but he also had a past. In 1959 the facade cracked. Longy Zwillman was named in the Senate Rackets Committee investigation of the juke-box industry, and shortly afterward he was found dead in his New Jersey home, apparently a suicide.

A curious example of underworld ethics occurred here in 1946 when Pauley Gibbons, a smalltime hoodlum, was ambushed and slain near his apartment on Gale Drive. Another detective and I attended funeral services for Gibbons at a mortuary chapel in a neighboring city. We were curious to see who would be among the mourners present, thinking that possibly we might find other "clients" there.

As we were sitting in silence, with the casket of the departed banked with flowers in the front of the chapel, and listening to soft music from the organ, there was a small commotion in the rear of the room. A newcomer had arrived with another box of flowers to add to the floral display. He was a ragged, unshaven and dirty "stew bum" who teetered slightly as he handed a long carton to the attending mortician. As the attendant took the box he noted it was unusually heavy for a "box of roses," and set it down in the rear of the room. After the services he asked us to inspect the package with him. It was decorated with a flossy card bearing this sentimental message: "To My Pal." The mortician unwrapped it carefully, fearing a bomb or other instrument of death. With utmost caution he lifted the lid and revealed the contents of the box. It was filled with horse manure.

This was a typical gesture of gangland defiance, a final slur to a dead enemy. We never located the sender. All the alcoholic messenger could remember was that somebody had given him $2 to deliver "a box of roses" to the funeral. We picked up two suspects in the Gibbons murder and held them for four days of questioning, but could not get a complaint against them. A short time later both men were killed in gangland fashion on Beverly Boulevard in Los Angeles.

As I've said before, the ways of the underworld are peculiar.

fourteen

WHO KILLED

BUGSY SIEGEL?

THE MURDER OF BENJAMIN (BUGSY) SIEGEL, THE ONLY big-time gangland killing in Beverly Hills, was an event we did not deserve. At the time, Siegel lived in Las Vegas, where he ran the multi-million dollar Flamingo Hotel and casino, and was only visiting our city. But gangsters have a prudent habit of staging their executions far away from the scene of their activities and chose Beverly Hills as a convenient spot to rub out Bugsy.

The slaying had everything to make it a sensation: a fusillade of shots through the window of a mansion home rented by a red-headed mystery woman; an underworld struggle for power in the gambling business; rumors of Siegel's link with the international narcotics traffic; and it also involved Hollywood, since the handsome, 42-year-old mobster had been popular in certain social circles where he had been introduced by his good friend, the fabulous Countess Dorothy di Frasso.

The fun-loving Countess was the darling of the film colony

for many years, and her gay adventures in cafe society made headlines in Europe and America. Her parties were command performances, and handsome leading men like Gary Cooper and Cary Grant followed in her train. She was the daughter of a New York millionaire, who acquired a title in 1923 by way of marriage to an Italian nobleman, Count Carlo di Frasso, and later lived high on the income from a $1,000,000 trust fund left by her father.

I never met the gay Countess on her many visits to Beverly Hills, but I knew Bugsy Siegel and his background. He was a gangster from Hell's Kitchen in New York, closely tied in with Louis (Lepke) Buchalter, Meyer Lansky, Frankie Yale, Joe Adonis, Jake (Gurrah) Shapiro, Abe (Kid Twist) Reles and other underworld figures. The mob specialized in fur-industry rackets, spread into the cleaning and dyeing field, and even into the poultry distributing business. Siegel and Meyer Lansky were reputed to be "trigger men" or "torpedoes" for the mob, which at one time was also associated with Charles (Lucky) Luciano in the prostitution racket.

In 1936, when Thomas E. Dewey lowered the boom on the New York mobsters, Siegel and his pals left town. Siegel came to California and bought a palatial 35-room home near Beverly Hills, reporting that his business interests required his presence on the West Coast. He set up as the top underworld figure in Southern California, and soon was suspected of engaging in the narcotics traffic between Mexico and the United States. He was also active in gambling combines and a racetrack wire service.

Suave and well-mannered, Bugsy posed as a polite, dapper man-about-town and "sportsman." Like all gangsters he was a big spender and lived in high style. He was quickly taken up by the Countess di Frasso, who was fascinated by the fact that she had a real live mobster in her social set, and introduced him into the top strata of Hollywood life. Always a charming fellow around the ladies, Siegel would not permit vile or abusive language in their presence, and dropped his nickname "Bugsy" in favor of the more dignified "Ben,"

140

although his underworld associates ignored the change in names. (He earned the name "Bugsy" by his habit of going berserk whenever he lost his temper.) He did not use narcotics himself, drank sparingly, and kept in good physical condition by daily workouts and massages at the gymnasium of the old Beverly Hills Athletic Club, where he spent much of his time.

In September of 1938, Siegel and Countess di Frasso and a few Hollywood friends sailed from San Pedro on the three-masted schooner *Metha Nelson* for a cruise to the tropics in search of shark oil, treasure and fun. (The 150-foot ship had been used in the movie "Mutiny on the Bounty.") The cruise turned out to be a comic opera adventure which ended four months later in wild charges of mutiny aboard a "hell ship," and a Federal grand jury investigation.

The leader of the expedition was Marino Bello, stepfather of the late Jean Harlow, and on the third day at sea the captain performed a marriage service for Bello and his fiancée, Evelyn Husby. Siegel acted as best man, the Countess was matron of honor, and all hands enjoyed a champagne party afterwards.

Bello had expected to finance the trip by catching 150 sharks a day and selling the oil to Germany. But as the weeks went by very few sharks were caught and the party decided to try treasure-hunting instead. The schooner dropped anchor at Cocos Island and everybody went ashore to dig for buried gold, but all they found were some old shovels used by other expeditions.

Homeward bound, after two months at sea, the treasure-hunters ran into a tropical storm in the Gulf of Tehuantepec and were drifting helplessly, with engine disabled and main-mast torn away, when they were sighted by an Italian liner, *S.S. Cellina*, and towed to Acapulco for repairs. Later the battered schooner continued northward to Ensenada, where Siegel and the Countess disembarked and finished the trip to Los Angeles by automobile, along with Richard Gulley, a Hollywood figure said to be a cousin of Sir Anthony Eden.

When the schooner reached its home port a Federal grand jury launched an investigation into charges of mutiny made by the skipper against two crew members. He testified that the crew was an unruly group of thugs, that he had had to put one man in chains and fight another, and that Countess di Frasso had feared she was going to be kidnapped. The Countess and other members of the party hotly denied the skipper's account and the charges were dismissed. One of the crewmen involved was Harry (Champ) Segal, a New York police character, who later was indicted along with Bugsy for the gangland slaying of Harry (Big Greenie) Greenberg, and freed.

Some of Siegel's glamour was dimmed in 1940 when he was arrested for the Greenberg murder. Greenberg, a former New York mobster, had threatened to squeal on Murder, Inc., and was shot down on a Hollywood street. When the District Attorney's investigators arrived at Siegel's home to arrest him they found him hiding in the attic. He had seen them outside the house, assumed they were rival gangsters, and climbed up through a trapdoor. Officers also found two safes hidden behind sliding panels in Siegel's mansion.

Two of his former New York associates, Abe Reles and Al Tannenbaum, told the County grand jury they had heard Siegel promise to "take care of" Greenberg. Later, Abe Reles, the key witness against Murder, Inc., in New York, was killed in a "fall" from a hotel window, much to the relief of several political leaders in that city.

Siegel's stay in County Jail caused a shakeup in the management when it was discovered that he had made eighteen trips outside the jail in two months for business and pleasure, including one lunch with a movie actress in a Wilshire Boulevard cafe, and that he had been a pampered guest of the jail hospital, with free telephone service, while he was supposed to be in durance vile. Other prisoners reported that Bugsy, always the dandy, had his tailor whip up a prison uniform for him of soft denim, and employed a fellow prisoner as valet to shine his shoes every morning. Siegel was tried in Superior Court for murder, but, as often happens in such cases involving top underworld figures, the charges eventually were dismissed.

When World War II started Bugsy was ready. He launched a small manufacturing plant in Los Angeles and got a rating as an essential industry, thus assuring himself and several of his mobster pals of gainful employment during the hostilities. At the same time he lived it up in Hollywood night clubs with Virginia Hill, a mystery woman with an unlimited bank roll. Miss Hill, a bosomy redhead, usually carried enough $100 bills to choke a horse and spent them like water on entertainment. She tossed a $7500 party for her friends at the Mocambo which aroused the interest of police because no one knew where her money came from. It was generally believed that Siegel was keeping an eye on her for one of his associates, a Brooklyn gambler.

At the end of the war, Las Vegas lured Siegel away from Hollywood and into new ventures which eventually led to his death. He decided to build the biggest and best gambling casino in the United States, financing it with syndicate money put up by his eastern pals, and to expand his "bootleg" racing wire service to take over the western part of the country.

He launched construction of his big casino when materials were scarce and costs soaring. He had originally planned a $2,000,000 investment, but found the place costing $6,000,-000, and running in the red. He put the squeeze on his other activities for funds, particularly the racing wire service. After the gangland murder in 1946 of James M. Ragen, general manager in Chicago of the Trans-America News Service in which Siegel had a controlling interest, he became western representative of the wire and attempted to force bookies to take his service at a premium in order to help meet expenses at the hotel.

As Siegel went deeper into debt, word got around that his syndicate pals were unhappy. Six months before his killing I talked to him in my office and reminded him that I did not want anything unpleasant happening in Beverly Hills.

143

His answer was that there was no need to worry because he was spending his time in Las Vegas.

When I was in New York a few months later on police business, I picked up the information that he had been in the city for a meeting with the men who controlled the money, and had left in haste. It was felt that his number was up. His hotel was reportedly $3,000,000 in the red, and Siegel had told friends he had to raise $1,500,000 in 30 days to pull it out of the hole. I did not know it at the time but Beverly Hills had already been chosen as the spot for his execution.

Three months before the killing his red-haired girl friend, Virginia Hill, rented a handsome 16-room home on North Linden Drive, which was owned by Juan Romero, former manager of Rudolph Valentino. Bugsy had a gold key to the front door, kept some of his clothes and a .38 caliber automatic in an upstairs room, and stayed at the house on his one or two-day business trips to our city.

June 20, 1947, was Siegel's last day alive. He flew in from Las Vegas at 4 A.M. and checked in at Miss Hill's residence. She had left town a few days previously on a trip to New York and Paris, and, since her lease was expiring, Siegel intended to pick up his things and take them back to Las Vegas with him.

In the afternoon he met his white-haired associate, Allen Smiley, who drove him to a barber shop and made a dinner date with him for the evening. Later, Siegel visited his attorney on business, returning to the Hill residence at 7:30 P.M. to meet Smiley and their dinner companions, Charles Hill, 21-year-old brother of Virginia, and Jeri Mason, her secretary, both of whom lived in the house.

The foursome drove to Ocean Park for a trout dinner and returned home at 10:15 P.M. Siegel and Smiley went into the living room and sat side by side on the davenport to read early editions of the Los Angeles morning newspapers. At 10:45 P.M. a series of shots crashed through the living-room window. Smiley dived to the floor unharmed, but Siegel did not move. He had been killed almost instantly by the first two bullets, which struck him in the head. Two other bullets had lodged in his body. He lay back on the davenport, his hands resting in his lap, with a newspaper between his grotesquely sprawled legs.

Other bullets had thudded into the wall, wrecked a statuette of Pan and punctured a painting of a nude holding a wine glass. Nine shells were found in the driveway of the house next door. The killer had rested his high-caliber rifle in a latticed pergola a dozen feet from where Siegel and Smiley sat. No one saw the gunman escaping, but a visitor in the neighborhood heard the shots and rushed outside in time to hear a car being driven rapidly up North Linden Drive toward Sunset Boulevard.

On the day Siegel was killed I was in New York City picking up a criminal who was involved in a $150,000 jewel robbery of a society matron. Only a few hours before the murder my prisoner staunchly maintained his innocence, using Siegel as his alibi. He swore that Bugsy had seen him at the Flamingo in Las Vegas on the day the Beverly Hills hold-up was committed.

Bugsy Siegel's killing was a perfectly staged gangland execution, with all the details worked out in advance. Somebody knew that Siegel would be in Beverly Hills on this one day, and that he would be at Virginia Hill's home, and when. Somehow the heavy draperies over the living-room window had been left open to give the killer a view of the room. The shooting was timed exactly to occur when no police patrol car was near, and had to be done quickly since police cars were in the vicinity every 30 minutes. The gunman at the window was hidden from the street by shrubbery, and the getaway car cruised the area until the appointed time, since a parked car might have drawn suspicion.

We spent many man-hours investigating the Siegel case and were convinced that he was killed by his own associates, but there was never sufficient evidence to pinpoint the identity of the assassins. I felt it was significant that Moe Sedway, a man with a police record, walked into the Flamingo to take over the operation for the syndicate one hour after Siegel's death, 300 miles away. At my first opportunity, I picked up Sedway for questioning and released him with word that I wanted to see him on the following day. However, he was suddenly removed to a Hollywood hospital for treatment for a heart condition. I found him there next day lying in bed behind a door marked "No Admittance—Oxygen!" I stepped in and talked briefly to Sedway, and left with word that I would return in the morning. But when morning came I discovered that the sick man had been put on a train and whisked off to Las Vegas, where he stayed until his death by natural causes a short time later. I have always felt that Moe Sedway had the information I wanted, but he wouldn't talk.

About this time several newspaper articles mentioned that I was investigating Las Vegas angles in the Siegel killing, a fact which annoyed the then Chief of Police of the Nevada city. He announced in a newscast that if he caught me in his city with a gun he would lock me up in jail, but his threat did not hinder our investigation. Later, the new operators of the Flamingo had a bitter battle, and one of them left the city in haste, under threat of death. I interrogated this man on his arrival in Beverly Hills, but he was reluctant to talk, fearing gangland retaliation. When I attempted to obtain more details on the fight in Las Vegas, I found that the District Attorney there was also the attorney for one of the combatants, a rather unusual situation.

Siegel was killed because he would not comply with the wishes of his associates who had invested millions in the Flamingo. My investigation tied him in with mobs in other cities and with international narcotics operators. I came across the trail of half a dozen other murders which were traceable to gangster and gambling connections. Only recently a former Las Vegas gambler, who had operated the Flamingo casino after Siegel's death, and his wife were mysteriously murdered in their home in Phoenix, Arizona. On the surface it did not appear to be a gangland killing, because Gus Greenbaum and his wife were found with their throats slit. But killers have been known to use unusual methods to avert suspicion from "the mob," and at close range a knife is as effective as a gun.

We did not see Virginia Hill again in Beverly Hills after Siegel was executed in her rented home. She was questioned about the killing in Paris, but denied all knowledge of it and couldn't think of anybody who might want to do in Siegel. When last heard from, she was spending most of her time in Mexico.

And the fun-loving Countess di Frasso, who sponsored the mobster's debut in Hollywood social circles, died as dramatically as she had lived a few years later. The Countess, aged 66 years, suffered a fatal heart attack on a train as she was returning to Los Angeles after a gay New Year's celebration in Las Vegas in January 1954. Clifton Webb, the actor, found her lying in her Pullman bedroom fully dressed, covered with a full-length mink coat, wearing a $175,000 diamond necklace, and with $100,000 worth of pearls and emeralds in her luggage. Friends said she always carried her jewelry with her everywhere.

fifteen

THE MAD BOMBER

OF BEVERLY HILLS

CHARLEY WAS A TOUGH, OLD HARD-ROCK MINER FROM Montana, with a weathered, deeply furrowed face and hands gnarled by years of work. He had never asked anything from anyone before except a job, but now he felt he had a claim against the State of California. He had been injured while working in a shipyard at Los Angeles Harbor, he said, and demanded monetary compensation. At his hearing before the State Industrial Accident Commission, Charley's claim was disallowed. Medical testimony established that his injury had actually been incurred years earlier in a mining accident in Montana.

Charley did not take this rejection lightly. In fact, he was enraged. He blamed the individual members of the Commission and the doctors personally, and set about to even up his score with them. Since Charley was what psychologists call the non-verbal type, he preferred direct action to words in settling arguments. In this case he chose dynamite.

Charley obtained the names and addresses of all the individuals involved in his hearing, some of them in Beverly Hills, and began plotting their immediate extinction. He purchased a large supply of dynamite and fuses in San Bernardino County, explaining that he needed the material for a mining project. In his Long Beach home, he fashioned a bomb for each of his intended victims, packing two-gallon Coca-Cola cans with dynamite sticks.

Before cutting his fuses, Charley rented an automobile and made a carefully-timed trip over the route covering his targets, seven homes in all. His plan was to cut the fuses in varying lengths, making the first ones long enough so that he would have sufficient time to plant bombs at all the houses and be safely out of the area before the first one exploded. If his scheme succeeded he would wipe out seven homes and 35 people, including some small children, and be on a freight train headed north before any suspicion could touch him.

On the night he put his plan in execution Charley loaded his home-made bombs in a rented truck and began his rounds. At 3 A.M. as he was placing a bomb under the window of a doctor's home, Charley was spotted by a Beverly Hills patrol car officer. The officer had seen Charley's truck parked by the curb and had stopped to investigate, since parking on the streets is not allowed between 2 A.M. and 6 A.M. Looking around, the officer saw the dim figure of a man in the doctor's yard and a fuse sparkling in the grass. He stamped out the fuse, arrested Charley and picked up the bomb. He led the old miner back to the truck where he found three more bombs, and hustled Charley and his truck off to the police station, parking the truck in a large open area 300 feet from the station.

As Charley was being interrogated by the lieutenant in charge of the morning watch a terrific explosion shook a wide area of Beverly Hills and the old miner fainted dead away. A bomb which he had planted a short time earlier had gone off as planned.

Awakened by the blast, I raced to headquarters shortly after the explosion. In searching the subject we found a list of names and addresses on him and sent out a general alarm to surrounding police forces to check the addresses. In Los Angeles, police checked the first two houses on Charley's list and found the other bombs the old miner had planted. Both had failed to explode because the morning dew had dampened the extra-long fuses. Had it not been for the heavy dew a dozen people would have been killed.

Charley's only victim in Beverly Hills, we discovered when we went to the scene, was an innocent bystander, Herman Hover, famous in Hollywood as the owner of Ciro's, a film colony night club. Hover had only recently moved into a house which had formerly been occupied by a doctor for the Industrial Accident Commission. The explosion lifted the house two inches off its foundation and blew a two-by-four timber through the ceiling of the bedroom, narrowly missing the occupants. Luckily, no one was injured.

Later in the morning Charley led us to a flood-control channel in Long Beach where he had tossed his leftover sticks of dynamite. On the way he appeared to be gleeful over his achievement. "I bet I scared hell out of that fellow," he chortled, "and the rest of them are scared too!"

At Charley's trial two psychiatrists presented conflicting testimony. One doctor said the old miner was just hot tempered, but the defense psychiatrist convinced the court that he was insane. Charley was committed to Mendocino State Hospital and kept there for a year while under observation by the medical and psychiatric staff. At the end of the year Charley went before the court seeking his release from the hospital. Under California law persons sentenced as insane can ask for a hearing after serving a year and be released if found sane.

Charley's sanity hearing was held in Superior Court at Ukiah, in the northern part of California. I flew there to protest his release, but my trip was in vain. According to the testimony of the hospital staff the old miner was sane, and some testified that he should not have been sent there in the first place. No one showed the slightest interest in Charley's demonstrated capacity for criminal violence. The court advised me that the only issue to be determined was whether the man was sane or not.

After his release from the mental hospital, we were tipped off that Charley was heading straight back to Los Angeles. Those of us responsible for his apprehension were ready for anything the brooding old bomber might have dreamed up to toss at us. But Charley apparently believed in first things first and went directly to the Industrial Accident Commission. His mission was fortunately non-violent and rather canny: Charley simply applied all over again for compensation for the old injury. Taking all the factors into consideration—which no doubt included a thought or two concerning the safety of life, limb and property—the Commission lost no time in granting a substantial settlement. Charley, along with all the rest of us, breathed easier. We took the precaution of keeping the homes of Beverly Hills members of the Commission under watch and hung his photograph in the "alert" section of our police bulletin board until this foxy old character got his money and left town. I heard that he panned a little gold in the Mother Lode country to keep himself busy and eventually went back to Montana where he died a few years later.

Old Charley was not the only man whose violent temper got him into trouble with the law. I remember vividly another who was Charley's opposite in every way. Handsome, dignified and well-dressed, he lived in the best hotels and apartments on an income of $3500 a month, yet he was subject to insane rages which made him a menace to the community.

When I first encountered him he had just wrecked an expensive apartment in a fit of vandalism. After a trivial argument with his landlady, he had purchased a quart bottle of black ink and smeared the contents over the rugs and draperies, leaving the place a shambles. The landlady called the police and I arrived to take him into custody. He seemed

151

normal enough when I began to question him, but something I said caused him to fly into a rage. He hurled a book at me, narrowly missing my head.

When we booked him at the station we found $7000 in cash and business checks on his person. We investigated and learned that he was a genius of the investment world who had amassed a sizeable fortune through his stock market operations. He had also left a trail of destruction and outraged landlords behind him at hotels and apartments where he had moved out after violent outbreaks. At one place he had slashed leather upholstery and draperies with a knife. Between tantrums he was a rational individual, but even then he worked off his spite by writing anonymous threatening letters to persons against whom he developed grudges.

We committed him to the psychopathic ward at the County Hospital for observation and at his sanity hearing the court ordered him committed to a private sanitarium, since he could well afford to pay for treatment. His lawyer requested a stay of execution to enable the man to select one of several exclusive private hospitals for his confinement. The attorney assured the court he would have a guard with his client at all times to keep him from violence.

A few days later, when the financial wizard was walking with his guard on Hollywood Boulevard he jumped into a passing taxicab and drove away, leaving the embarrassed guard standing on the sidewalk waving his arms. We sent out a general alarm, but we never saw the man again. Several years later we got an inquiry from authorities in New York State who were trying to locate his heirs. He had been found dead, and his fingerprints traced back to his arrest in Beverly Hills.

Mentally disturbed people are a constant problem to police. We probably see as many of them as psychiatrists do, because in many cases they feel that the police department can offer them protection from their imaginary dangers. During the years I have often had telephone calls from normal-sounding individuals who insist on a private interview with me to discuss their problems. Usually as they enter the office and begin talking they appear to be rational, but after a few minutes they begin to ramble and it becomes evident that they are mentally unbalanced.

I have had playwrights, song writers and inventors come to my office with wild stories about inventions and literary material stolen from them. I have listened to husbands who imagined their wives were trying to poison them, to women who think they are being trailed by mysterious men, and to financiers who describe imaginary deals in which they say they have been defrauded out of large sums of money.

The most recent case I recall was a onetime prominent doctor who walked into my office unannounced and requested permission to use my private telephone. He confided that he was on a highly secret assignment. He had been chosen as one of the crew for the first rocket trip to the moon and, consequently, was being watched night and day by "the enemy." They had tapped his telephone and were listening to all his conversations, but he felt my private line would be safe to use. I assured him I would help him get on the rocket ship, but in the meantime I made arrangements for his confinement in a private hospital.

I have learned to expect the unexpected in police work. I once solved a murder, inadvertently, by doing a kindness for a man I had sent to prison. Yet my action surprisingly set off a chain of circumstances which sent him to his death on the gallows. He was a tough customer whom we had in jail for burglary in 1937. His name was Wilbur J. Smith, and he had hit eight homes in Beverly Hills, including the residence of Alice Faye, screen star. He was known as a cat burglar. His method was to creep into a wealthy home and hide under a bed where he would wait for the occupants of the house to retire for the night. Sometimes he watched them undress. After everyone was asleep, Smith would quietly crawl out from his hiding place, pick up all the money and jewelry, and sneak out of the house.

Overconfidence was his downfall. One night he got a

little careless in a Beverly Hills home and went to sleep on the thick carpet of a luxurious master bedroom while he was waiting for the owners to return from a late party. They arrived sooner than he had anticipated and found him snoring heartily under their bed. They quietly summoned police and a patrol car brought him to jail.

I had almost nabbed him a month earlier when he was seen running out of a house, but he leaped into a waiting automobile and escaped. We found the car abandoned in Hollywood and traced him to a Hollywood hotel where he had registered under a fictitious name. As I entered the front door of the hotel to get him, he went out a rear window and got away. Since we were familiar with his *modus operandi,* we knew we had our man when the patrol car brought in the sleeping burglar.

Smith was put in a cell with a blind man while awaiting trial. One night when I was the lieutenant in charge of the late watch I heard a deathly yell in the cell block. I was used to the noise made by drunks in the tank, but this was different, a desperate shout. Hurrying out of my office I reached the booking desk just in time to see Smith running out into the corridor with a sergeant in pursuit. Taking a different angle from the sergeant, I pursued the fleeing burglar across the City Hall lawn and fired a shot which hit him in the leg. We handcuffed him and brought him back to the jail where we found the dazed jailer nursing a knot on his head the size of a golf ball.

The jailer told us he had been putting the prisoners to bed for the night when Smith got his blind cellmate to stumble and fall in front of him. As the officer leaned over to help the blind man Smith slugged him viciously on the head and ran.

Some weeks later, after the burglar had been sent to State Prison at San Quentin, I noticed that his automobile was still in storage in the police garage. I wrote him a letter suggesting that he sell the car before storage charges ate up its value, and volunteered to handle the transaction for him.

154

Smith replied promptly, asking me to sell the car and deposit the proceeds to his account at San Quentin. A mother bought the car for her son in college and I forwarded the money, several hundred dollars, to San Quentin for Smith.

The burglar thanked me warmly for this service, but in his criminal mind he was plotting a nefarious use for the money. To a cellmate who was about to be released from prison Smith confided that he wanted to clear up an unpleasant situation in Sacramento. He had killed a man there during a burglary some months earlier and the murder had been witnessed by a housemaid who could identify Smith. She had seen Smith in the act of burglarizing a house and had summoned a neighbor to capture him, but Smith shot and killed the man when he confronted him. Later he had disposed of the murder weapon by dropping it overboard into the Pacific Ocean during a boat trip from Los Angeles to Santa Catalina Island.

The maid was the only witness. If she could be done away with, Smith's worries would be over. He offered the automobile money to his cellmate to kill the maid. The cellmate, however, was eager to obtain his own release as soon as possible and secretly had qualms about committing murder. He repeated Smith's story to the warden, who dispatched officers to Sacramento to bring the maid to the prison. The woman quickly identified Smith as the murderer and he was shortly thereafter tried, convicted and sentenced to death. He was one of the last, if not the last man to be legally hanged in California before the State installed a gas chamber for executions.

This was the unexpected outcome of my good deed, a murder solved by kindness and a murderer hanged on the gallows.

sixteen

CHARLIE CHAPLIN'S

GIRL FRIEND

SHORTLY BEFORE MIDNIGHT ON THE LAST DAY OF 1942 a red-haired, freckled young woman stormed into the Beverly Hills police station and announced her intention of sleeping in jail. Her name was Joan Berry, she said, age 23. She had just had a fight with her "boy friend," who had let her out of his car across the street from the station, telling her to "sleep in the jail." She was broke and had nowhere else to go.

The lieutenant in charge of the morning watch and a policewoman listened to the young woman's story and explained that they could not lock her up for the night unless she were a vagrant. The officers suggested that their uninvited guest try to think of somebody else who would offer her shelter. After sitting in the station for an hour and a half, she remembered that she had a friend on Olympic Boulevard and an officer and the policewoman delivered her at an apartment house at the address given.

A few hours later an unidentified man telephoned headquarters to report that a woman was committing suicide on

156

Olympic Boulevard. Officers and an ambulance, dispatched to the scene, found Miss Berry seated in an automobile in front of the apartment. She was scantily clad in a man's pajamas and had iodine smeared around her mouth. She had taken poison, she said, and had already notified the newspapers. In fact, a reporter was waiting with her when the ambulance arrived. She was rushed to the emergency hospital for treatment, but the examining doctor could find no trace of poison. It was obvious that she was faking suicide.

Since she claimed to have no home, no money and no means of support, she was placed in custody on a vagrancy charge. She was wearing a man's bathrobe, pajamas and slippers when she was booked, but she had changed her mind about wanting to sleep in the jail. When prison clothes were given her in the women's quarters she refused to put on the uppers, and paraded in front of the matron half nude. Her vanity case was taken away after she broke its mirror and threatened to cut her wrists with the glass.

Detectives questioned her later in the morning and learned, to their great surprise, that the "boy friend" who was the target of her fake suicide was one of the most famous men in our city, Charlie Chaplin. Although the white-haired comedian, 54 years old at the time, had been a celebrated resident of Beverly Hills for many years, Chaplin was only a name to most of us. He lived on a large hilltop estate near Pickfair in a castle-like house almost completely hidden by trees. We knew he had an excellent tennis court, where "Big Bill" Tilden, the former tennis champion, played regularly, but we seldom saw him on the streets of the city. The only time we had him in the police station he was brought to the emergency hospital for first-aid treatment. He had locked himself out of his castle and cut his leg when he kicked open a glass door to get in.

Although he was one of the wealthiest men in the motion-picture industry and internationally famous, Chaplin was generally unpopular in the film colony because of his failure to become an American citizen and his apparently hostile attitude toward public opinion. He did not participate in community activities and was not noted for either philanthropy or public spirit. His political ideas seemed to come out of left field, and his lofty statements that he was a "paying guest" and not a "nationalist" sounded almost unfriendly to his American fans. Even after more than 40 years residence here Chaplin considered himself an international figure rather than an American. His one-man war against public opinion boomeranged on him in the Joan Berry case.

Miss Berry's link with Chaplin was confirmed on the day after her arrest when she pleaded guilty to vagrancy and received a 90-day sentence, suspended on condition she discontinue her disorderly conduct. When it was learned that she was badly in debt to a fashionable hotel, a spokesman for Chaplin volunteered to pay her hotel bill and her transportation home. This offer seemed to be a humane and logical solution to Miss Berry's difficulties at the time, and a few days later she boarded an eastbound train.

But five months later Miss Berry was back with us and in trouble. Tim Durant, an actor friend of Chaplin's, called the police department to report that she was creating a disturbance at the comedian's home, where she was trying to break in. She was arrested for violating the terms of her probation and taken to the County Jail. This time, however, she had an announcement to make that rallied the anti-Chaplin forces to her defense and got her out of jail after one day. Chaplin, she said, was the father of her unborn child.

Miss Berry's story was headlined in newspapers everywhere. She had first met Chaplin in 1941, she said, and he had promised her fame and fortune in the films. He put her under personal contract at $100 a week and devoted his time to training her. "I spent many evenings with Mr. Chaplin at his home," she said. "We studied Shakespeare together— 'Antony and Cleopatra' and the sonnets. Mr. Chaplin coached me in diction, speech, voice control, voice projection and all the other technical dramatic arts." Later the comedian's interest in her had cooled, she said, and her contract had ex-

158

pired in October, 1942. She found herself flat broke, and, after her arrest for vagrancy, left town with a railroad ticket to New York and $100 in cash provided by Chaplin. But when the train reached Omaha she had decided to get off and return to California. "Mr. Chaplin was very much surprised to see me again," she reported, which was probably an understatement.

Overnight Miss Berry became a symbol of the public's resentment of Chaplin. A number of Hollywood personalities and newsmen took up her case, arranged legal representation for her, and placed her in a sanitarium. Her vagrancy sentence was modified in the interest of "social justice," and several days later attorneys for her mother filed a paternity suit against Chaplin in behalf of the unborn child. Chaplin vigorously denied responsibility, and agreed to let science determine the paternity of the child through blood tests to be made of himself and the baby not less than four months after birth.

In June of 1943, while the paternity suit was still pending, Chaplin surprised everybody by eloping with Oona O'Neill, 18-year-old daughter of Playwright Eugene O'Neill. When newsmen and photographers got wind of his plans, Chaplin and his bride-to-be eluded them in a 70-mile-an-hour automobile chase along the Coast Highway to Carpinteria, California, where they were married with only several friends as witnesses.

Miss Berry's baby, a daughter named Carol Ann, was born in October, 1943. Blood tests made of Chaplin and the baby four months later indicated that he could not be the father because of the difference in their blood types. Steps were taken to dismiss Miss Berry's paternity suit, in accordance with the prior agreement between attorneys for both parties. But at this point the famous criminal lawyer Joe Scott of Los Angeles leaped into the Chaplin-Berry case. He charged that the blood test agreement was invalid because it did not give the baby her day in court, and that the mother could not forfeit the child's rights. Superior Judge Stanley

Mosk, now California's Attorney-General, upheld Scott's contention and denied dismissal of the paternity suit.

Meanwhile, Chaplin was battling on another legal front. A Federal indictment charged him with two violations of the Mann Act on the complaint of Miss Berry that he had transported her to New York and back to Hollywood for immoral purposes, and another indictment accused him of "conspiracy" in removing her from Beverly Hills. The conspiracy charge was dismissed for lack of evidence, but the Mann Act trial was a two-week sensation in Los Angeles Federal Court.

Defended by Jerry Giesler, Chaplin took the stand to tell of his hectic romance with Miss Berry. He testified that he had had to change the locks on his doors four times because she stole the keys, and that on one occasion after he had refused her entrance he found her lying on the mat outside his front door. A week before Miss Berry's dramatic entrance at the Beverly Hills police station, he said, she had confronted him in his bedroom with a gun and walked around the beds threatening to kill him, after breaking two windows to gain entrance. Miss Berry's version of the incident was slightly different. She said that she had intended to kill herself, not Chaplin, with a .25 caliber Spanish type pistol which she had purchased from a Hollywood gun shop a few days earlier. After their final battle, Chaplin had driven her in his car to the Beverly Hills City Hall and told her to "Go sleep in the police station."

It was also established that Miss Berry had boasted of her association with other influential and financially prominent men elsewhere in the United States. Although Chaplin had given Miss Berry and her mother tickets to New York, and later had met her there at a hotel, the jury decided he had not taken her there for immoral purposes and he was acquitted.

There was still another year to go on the Chaplin-Berry case, and two civil trials, probably the lengthiest litigation of its kind in local history. The first paternity trial ended in January, 1945, with a hung jury, and the second trial, four

160

months later, resulted in a jury decision that Chaplin was the father of the child. He was ordered by the court to provide support for the child. He carried the case to the United States Supreme Court the following year, but lost his appeal.

The Chaplin case again focused the attention of the world on Hollywood morals, and one scandal goes a long way to besmirch the entire community. However, in my 30 years here I have found that the leading stars and the important people in the motion-picture and television industry are seldom in trouble with the law. Usually, they're too busy. They work long hours at the studios, and rest at night and on weekends. The scandals which develop here generally start among those whose careers are on the wane, or perhaps never got started, or among playboys who have plenty of leisure time to get into devilment.

Scandal magazines and newspaper stories make the most of every incident because of the international prominence of the names involved, with the result that the picture given of film colony life is often more exaggerated than factual. Very seldom has any important motion-picture personality been in trouble with the police on a serious charge. I can't remember half a dozen really prominent people of this community who have been in the City Jail, except as visitors, in all my years on the force. Often the individuals who get the headlines in this type of Hollywood news are "extras," or men and women who have at one time or another worked long enough on movie sets to identify themselves as "actors."

Most of the headline action here is in the divorce courts, and unfortunately there are many cases of marital discord involving temperamental actors and actresses, beautiful people who decide they can no longer stay together. But this is a problem which is nationwide and for which I have no solution to offer.

In the Chaplin case, even though he was at fault he was a victim of public opinion which convicted him in advance on the report of an unscrupulous individual. There was even criticism of the police department's handling of Miss Berry's

161

case, as if our action was taken for the purpose of shielding Chaplin. However, the young woman's misconduct would have made her arrest and sentencing mandatory in any city, regardless of who else was involved.

Shortly after winning the paternity suit, Miss Berry left California to live in the East where she married again. Nine years later she was found wandering barefoot about the streets of Torrance, California, and was committed to a State hospital. Her 10-year-old daughter, central figure in the suit, had been put in a private boarding school where other students were unaware of her identity.

In September 1952, Charlie Chaplin and his young wife and their children sailed for Europe, leaving behind a great coolness which had grown up between the comedian and the American public. Soon after Chaplin left the country the United States Attorney-General announced that he could not re-enter without a hearing in regard to "moral turpitude" and his alleged Communist sympathies. Chaplin, in reply, vowed he would never return.

The former Chaplin estate on Summit Drive has since been subdivided and holds several modern homes. Only old-timers remember its location and what it used to look like. And they also remember Charlie Chaplin when he was an amusing little fellow on the screen, with derby hat, bamboo cane, baggy pants and oversize shoes, and wish that this talented comedian could have retained more of this innocent charm in his private life.

seventeen

FATHER DIVINE'S "HEAVEN"—

BEVERLY HILLS BRANCH

THE TIME WAS NOVEMBER, 1936, AND THE VOICE ON the telephone at police headquarters was familiar to millions around the world. "What the devil's going on across the street from my house?" Lionel Barrymore wanted to know. The dean of America's most famous acting family then delivered a few more pungent comments concerning events in the 800 block on North Roxbury Drive and asked what the police department was going to do. His call was no surprise to us. A dozen or more of his neighbors had already called to report unusual activity at one of the finest homes in the neighborhood, and patrol officers had observed scores of cars parking and crowds of people coming and going. We advised Mr. Barrymore that we were investigating and would take action if it were warranted.

We watched the place for two days to make sure of our position. It was in a quiet and exclusive street, and highly restricted, yet to all appearances a small convention was in progress. Between 150 and 250 people were gathering there daily, with accompanying sounds of speechmaking and social clamor. Much to our surprise we discovered that several disciples of Father Divine, the spectacular Harlem religious leader, had established a new "heaven" in a large and expensive mansion, and were inviting the faithful to attend from far and near.

When the shouting and unnecessary noise became too much, on the night of November 15, Captain W. W. White and I went to the front door of the mansion and asked for the leader. The house was teeming with a mixed group of people, and finally a pathway was cleared for a fat, rosy-cheeked blonde young man, about 30 years old and weighing 220 pounds, who stepped forward and introduced himself solemnly as St. John the Divine.

We found his impressive title hard to believe, since we hadn't heard of any recent reincarnation, but we proceeded to advise him that he would have to discontinue his meetings because he was violating the zoning law and disturbing the peace. His followers milled around us as we gave our ultimatum, and St. John bounced up the stairs to a second-floor landing where he stopped dramatically, spoke some words of mumbo-jumbo, and asked the crowd with a gesture to be silent while he meditated. After a brief pause, he rattled off some more gibberish and announced, eloquently, that he had been in direct communication with Father Divine and "the spirits," who had advised him to disregard our order.

I told the assembled disciples that regardless of this spiritual guidance from afar their meeting was an unlawful assembly and we would find it necessary to arrest them unless they dispersed. At this the crowd became unruly and threatening, but simmered down when Captain White summoned additional police cars to the scene by radio. As our reinforcements arrived the crowd began leaving the premises.

We arrested the three leaders and took them to the police station for booking on charges of committing a public nuisance. At the station all three gave us fanciful names and listed their home address as 20 West 115th Street, New York

164

City, which was Father Divine's headquarters. St. John, who also used the names of John the Revelator and Jesus the Christ, claimed his age was "two days," since he had just been reborn the day before, thanks to Father Divine. The second man, who gave his name as Socrates, was carrying $7000 in greenbacks in his pocket, a startling amount of money for this depression era. The third man, who claimed to be Ben Jamin or John the Baptist, had $2281.86 in his pockets.

We also learned their true identities. St. John was the son of a wealthy Cleveland, Ohio, industrialist and had taken over his widowed mother's Beverly Hills home for his "religious" activities. Socrates was his younger brother, and white-haired Ben Jamin, whose real name was Smith, was his aide-de-camp. Ben Jamin warned me solemnly that a judge in Long Island had died mysteriously three days after sentencing Father Divine in a New York case. The same fate awaited me, he said, for daring to defy the unknown powers of "The Father."

At the trial of the three disciples in Beverly Hills Municipal Court the record became so full of New Testament names that it was confusing. Disciples would attend a session as spectators, then take the stand as witnesses on the following day and change names. "Mary Magdalene" announced that she had been reborn during the day and was now "Martha," and a "St. Paul" became "St. John." They all gave their ages as anywhere from one day to two years, according to the time they claimed "rebirth." However, Lionel Barrymore and other citizens gave testimony which made sense, the defendants were convicted of disturbing the peace, and the "heaven" was closed, never to reopen.

I warned St. John's mother to keep an eye on all the expensive personal property in her home, but, after the visiting disciples left, silverware and other valuables were missing. The mother had joined the Divine sect with the name of "Mary Bird Tree" and thousands of dollars had literally and figuratively been shaken from her. I still remember my last

165

view of the dining room in her home. Fourteen chairs stood around a large oval table, with one chair holding a huge picture of Father Divine, about three by four feet in size. During their feasts the disciples had always left this chair vacant, but they would talk to the picture and leave food on a plate in front of it to keep "The Father" happy.

During the trials some of the members of the sect obtained my home telephone number and would ring me at intervals during the night, warning me that I was a doomed man, or that my house was going to be burned. But since "crank" calls are just one of the normal hazards of a policeman's lot, I disregarded them.

We learned more amazing facts about the self-proclaimed St. John and his local "heaven" when he was picked up later by Federal authorities on Mann Act charges involving one of his young female disciples. At this trial he testified that he had visited Father Divine in the latter's "Promised Land" at Kingston, New York, and started westward to spread the message. Accompanied by two other disciples he made the trip in a luxurious Duesenberg sedan, stopping enroute for "high class meetings and swell banquets." In Denver, Colorado, he picked up a 17-year-old girl to whom he gave the "heavenly name" of "Mary Dove," transporting her to Beverly Hills to be "the second Virgin Mary," destined to bring into the world a "new Redeemer." He said he chose her for this honor because he saw lights around her when he first met her in Denver, and later she lit up on occasions in his Beverly Hills home. He outfitted her in a set of flowing robes with her badge of rank, and stayed at various hotels with her, registered as "Jesus the Christ" and "The Virgin Mary," with a modest "no publicity" notation written after each name.

When he urged "Mary Dove" to go to a desert island with him and bear a child, she simply didn't want to. All she wanted really was to get in the movies. Disillusioned, St. John took her with him on another transcontinental automobile trip to visit Father Divine in Kingston, and sent her home to her parents after "The Father" chided him for his carryings-on.

St. John took his religious personification seriously. On his first trip West, after reaching the town of Grants, New Mexico, he began the custom of giving only left-handed handshakes, because, he said, "we wanted to be different." And he was subject to "vibrations" which hit him at unexpected times. Once on the outskirts of Ojai, California, he declared, a particularly hard vibration struck him. "My left hand took and crippled itself, and everybody called me Jesus," he reported.

He threw away thousands of dollars of his mother's money in a short time. While traveling in an automobile with Ben Jamin, he testified, he met a man on the road with four donkeys. He stopped the car and ordered his aide to give the man $100, "Because he is Joseph!" However, Ben only had $1000 bills with him, so the surprised pedestrian got one of them. Ben Jamin later was quoted as saying he had paid out between $35,000 and $50,000 for St. John during just four months of traveling in 1936, including $800 paid to a Denver merchant for a wardrobe for "Mary Dove."

St. John's story in court also revealed for the first time why there had been so much excitement on North Roxbury Drive before we closed up his "heaven." On November 13th, he testified, he became almost a soaring blimp when tremendous spiritual vibrations hit him, and he had "soared around, and cried and laughed" and tossed handfuls of greenbacks to the disciples gathered in his home, $10,000 in all. His faithful Ben Jamin verified this story of St. John's lavish largesse. Said he: "It was beautiful. John just stood there, a smile of ecstasy on his face, and threw more than $10,000 away— threw it all on the floor of the living-room. He just didn't want to have any contact with the stuff!"

When this happened the other disciples present also went into spasms of spiritual ecstasy and fell on the floor. But even with "the spirit" on them in full blast they did not fail to

167

scoop up the $1000 and $100 bills among which they fell. St. John testified, slyly, that were were only 60 people in the house on this occasion, but next day the crowd grew to 200. He said he didn't know whether they came to see him get vibrations or because he had tossed money on the floor the day before.

At the conclusion of his Federal trial St. John was sentenced to three years in prison, and had to leave Beverly Hills with his most ambitious project still uncompleted. This was a fantastic $25,000 "throne car" which he was having built for him in Pasadena. Twenty feet in length and powered with a 265-horsepower Duesenberg motor, the car was designed to carry ten people in state, with the center of the rear seat elevated as a throne for St. John. The ceiling was lined with white plush, studded with stars, and the windows were of crystal and star-shaped. At the push of a button a segment of the top slid back, revealing whoever was seated on the throne.

St. John had planned to ride through the streets of Beverly Hills in this "golden chariot" and use it to spread the word of Father Divine throughout California, but it was not to be. I never heard of him again after he entered the Federal Prison at McNeil Island.

eighteen

TROUBLE

IN PARADISE

NOBODY IN HIS RIGHT MIND WANTS TO LEAP INTO THE middle of a battle between a married couple. This can be dangerous. Too often an enraged husband or wife will start shooting without warning. Something about family fights seems to encourage gun play. Police have learned to handle them cautiously. Even in less violent marital disputes a peacemaker needs the wisdom of Solomon. We would prefer to steer clear of such entanglements, but sometimes warring couples toss their troubles right in our laps and we have no choice but to intervene.

When these incidents involve prominent citizens and the spotlight of publicity is turned on us our problem is magnified. Officially the police do not regard a domestic quarrel in Beverly Hills as any more important than one in Dubuque, but frequently our local family difficulties make front-page news across the nation. When Walter Wanger, the distinguished motion-picture producer, shot and wounded a Hollywood agent in December, 1951, we were invaded by newspaper reporters and photographers, television and radio men and their equipment, who established a beachhead at police headquarters and covered the case in breathless detail.

The Wanger incident occurred when the producer confronted his actress wife, Joan Bennett, and her agent in a parking lot across the street from my office. Angered by the man's association with Miss Bennett and fearing an estrangement from her, Mr. Wanger fired two shots from a .38 caliber revolver at the agent. One bullet struck him in the leg and hip and the other ricocheted off the actress's automobile. The agent was quickly removed to a hospital by Miss Bennett and a service station attendant. Mr. Wanger surrendered immediately to the police and was brought across the street to the jail. When I asked him why he had resorted to violence the producer replied, "I shot him because I thought he was breaking up my home."

Legal wheels moved briskly after Mr. Wanger was locked up on suspicion of assault with intent to commit murder. Jerry Giesler showed up to represent the producer, and Jake Ehrlich, famous San Francisco criminal lawyer, arrived in behalf of the wounded agent, who refused to sign a complaint. Since all three participants in the affray had attorneys, I called in the District Attorney, the late Ernest Roll, to sit in on the interrogation. Actor George Murphy and the Wangers' family pastor also arrived at the jail to talk with Mr. Wanger and his wife.

Because of his important position in the community the producer was aided by civic and religious leaders who joined in a plea to the court to show him leniency. The charge against him was reduced to assault with a deadly weapon and, a few months later, he was found guilty in a trial which lasted just six minutes.

Extreme consideration was shown Mr. Wanger because of public sympathy for him and he was permitted to serve his four-month sentence in the Sheriff's Wayside Honor Farm rather than in the County Jail. In view of the mild treatment he received for a serious offense, we of the police department were surprised, therefore, when his next picture, "I Want to Live," brought what we felt was discredit on law enforcement methods and glorified a vicious criminal, Mrs. Barbara Graham, who had been executed by the State of California for her part in the brutal murder of an elderly housewife. The film, based on a famous Los Angeles County case, purported to show that the Graham woman was innocent and that her conviction had been obtained by trickery. As a drama it was powerful enough to win an Academy Award for Susan Hayward, but in substance it was an unfair, untrue and biased attack on police methods.

Our next outbreak on the domestic front was more funny than serious, and quickly solved. It happened when the Oscar Levants had a stimulating little spat one night to which the police were invited by the neighbors on North Roxbury Drive. When we arrived at the Levant home we found the celebrated pianist and television star upstairs yelling that his wife had chased him there after hitting him with the heel of her slipper. His pert and pretty wife, June, indignantly denied his charges. "You don't see any bruises, do you?" she asked. But she had chased him upstairs, and what the neighbors heard were Oscar's yells as he hastily ascended. We calmed down the battling Levants and went on our way.

No police report was made on this minor incident, but two days later the metropolitan press descended on my office en masse with the story of the quarrel and asked confirmation of it. Since I learned long ago that news cannot be suppressed I verified the report. Somebody had called the newspapers with the story, but it was nobody in the police department. We do not publicize our minor skirmishes because from a police viewpoint they are unimportant.

L'affaire Levant, however, soon became public property. Thousands of Southern Californians heard about it from Mr. Levant himself who discussed it candidly on his television show and in the press. He had been wrongfully accused, he said, of being out with other women. "Any time I take another woman out it's only for coffee," he observed plaintively.

171

"The secret of marriage is that they murder you and then you apologize for it." Later the Levants kissed and made up.

The funniest aspect of the story was the reception given to newspaper reporters when they arrived at the Levant home. They were greeted at the door by one of the three bright daughters of the family who acted as welcoming committee and was obviously enjoying the excitement. "You should have heard it," she told her visitors. "It was a good fight! And you know something? I've got the whole thing on my tape recorder!"

On another memorable occasion an indignant wife armed herself with a bottle of black ink and followed her estranged husband and his current blonde girl friend into a large movie theater on Wilshire Boulevard. She roamed through the darkened auditorium from row to row until she located her quarry sitting romantically close together, absorbed in the drama unfolding on the screen. At an appropriately dramatic moment she uncorked the ink bottle, the large economy size, and hurled its contents at the blissful couple. Unfortunately, her aim was deplorable and she succeeded only in splattering ink over numerous other people in the vicinity. We arrested her at the theater amid considerable hubbub. Later, after promising to pay the cleaning bills of all the victims of her surprise attack, she was let off with a fine and an admonition.

In another domestic dispute to which I was invited in my official capacity I sat all night in the front room of a citizen's home, waiting for the possible reappearance of his ex-wife. Earlier in the evening the lady had shot five times through his front door with a rifle, splintering the door but missing her former husband. He had married again after a divorce, but his first wife was carrying on a campaign against him. Perhaps it was lucky for me that she did not return for more target practice that night.

Probably our most publicized marital dispute was the Mary Astor case. Miss Astor was living on Tower Road in Beverly Hills in 1936 when her diary rocked the nation's newspapers during her lawsuit against her ex-husband, Dr.

Franklyn Thorpe, for the custody of their daughter. The screen star charged that much of the diary was a forgery detailing affairs with other men. The document was never admitted into evidence or read in court because it had been mutilated. It was ordered impounded by Superior Judge Goodwin J. Knight, later Governor of California, and was burned when the child in the case reached the age of 21 years.

Our police patrol cars sometimes uncover evidence of a domestic crisis even before a suspected husband or wife knows about it. One patrol car cruising down an alley spotted a heavy cable running from a telephone pole into an apartment. Since the cable was much heavier than an ordinary telephone would require, the officers were curious about it. They traced the cable for two blocks and into a private home where they found it connected to concealed microphones in a breakfast room used by a supposedly happily married couple. One "bug" was hidden in a flower pot beside the breakfast table and the other in a heating vent. Watching the apartment at the other end of the line the officers observed a man entering the room daily but never sleeping there. They investigated and learned that he was a private detective who dropped in daily to change records on the recording machine and to check on whether the "bugs" were operating. Obviously somebody was trying to get evidence for a divorce case by illegal means. Neither husband nor wife would admit ownership of the apparatus, however, so the police department acquired $1500 worth of equipment free and 1000 feet of insulated wire.

Another time, officers saw a similar cable installed in an office building and traced it back to its source a block away. They discovered that an elderly husband, suspicious of his wife's men friends, had "bugged" her office just to keep tab on her during the day and listen in on her office flirtations. Again, nobody would acknowledge ownership of the equipment, and the police department acquired another handsome recording device worth about $1200.

You learn to be a realist in police work, and the longer

you are in it the more surprising things happen. In this case the elderly husband decided he would be lonesome without his wife. He forgot his suspicions, forgave her office flirtations, and they lived happily afterward.

I was once surprised by a visit from a distinguished-looking middle-aged man who came into my office and identified himself as a marriage counselor. "You may think this is funny," he said, "but I need help from you in solving my own marriage problem." He and his wife both had children by former marriages living with them and the basis of their problem was that each showed favoritism to his own offspring when family decisions had to be made. His problem was too deep for me, but as we talked it over he seemed to feel better for sharing it with a sympathetic listener.

Domestic fights in Beverly Hills have been particularly bitter where money is involved. I have known wealthy husbands and wives to ask for the arrest of each other on charges of stealing personal property, bank funds, jewelry or automobiles. Such accusations are usually only spite affairs which are settled in civil court and seldom reach the criminal calendar. Frequently warring couples bring charges of "kidnapping" against each other, charges which have to be settled by lawsuits to determine the custody of the youngsters.

Sometimes the police discover extracurricular domestic situations in odd ways. One day I got a telephone call from the male secretary of a nationally-known business man in our town. "Say, Chief," he said, "you probably will get a burglary report from a woman on Olympic Boulevard this afternoon. I just want you to know the facts about it first. My boss has been living there with a girl friend, but he decided to go back to his wife. He sent me to the apartment to pick up his clothing while the girl was away. When she returns she's going to notice a lot of things missing."

Two hours later the telephone rang with a call from a woman who wanted to report a burglary at her apartment. I sent a detective to interview her and admonished him to ask her for a complete list, itemized, of everything missing.

174

The detective followed instructions and, as the woman listed her losses, noticed that everything she mentioned was an item of men's wearing apparel. As the list grew longer the officer interrupted her recital to ask: "Are you a married woman?" When she replied that she was unmarried he immediately wanted to know why she had so much men's wear in her apartment. As the woman fumbled for an answer the officer volunteered the information that there is a State law against adultery. "I certainly hope you don't have a man living here with you," he concluded helpfully. After thinking the situation over the woman decided she hadn't lost a thing —and another Beverly Hills crisis was solved.

nineteen

ROBBERS

FOR HIRE

THE MOST VICIOUS ROBBERY WE EVER HAD IN BEVERLY Hills occurred in an apartment house near Romanoff's. The victim was a wealthy matron who loved expensive jewelry and displayed it on her person at exclusive restaurants and night clubs, usually sitting at prominent tables where the sparkle would show.

One morning two bandits wearing hats and gloves, with masks made of black stockings pulled over their faces, rang the bell at her apartment. As the maid opened the door the men pushed their way inside at gunpoint and forced the girl to sit down in a chair and be silent. When the lady of the house appeared they held guns on her and ordered her to hand over her jewelry. After ransacking her dresser drawers of $125,000 worth of jewelry the bandits demanded to know what she had done with her most valuable ring, an 18-carat diamond worth $30,000. The frightened woman replied that it was in a wall safe in the master bedroom, but that she did not know the combination. Angered, the men pistol-whipped her until her face was covered with blood. But she still insisted that she could not open the safe. She was to spend two weeks in the hospital as a result of this beating. Finally, after locking the matron and her maid in a closet, the bandits departed with their loot.

This robbery perplexed us. The two robbers had obviously been informed that the woman was the owner of an expensive diamond ring. The previous owner was a movie star who had been squeezed out in the stock market and needed cash. Six months before the robbery it had been offered to the victim by a jewelry firm operated by two enterprising brothers on Wilshire Boulevard, but she had turned the 18-carat diamond down and purchased the same ring later from another jeweler for a lower price. We soon learned through an underworld tip that the brothers were the villains in this scheme.

Angered because their wealthy customer had by-passed them in purchasing the diamond, they had contacted two gunmen in New York City and brought them to Los Angeles to plot revenge on the woman. They kept the hoods in a hotel for several weeks while waiting for their intended victim to return from a vacation on the Arizona desert. It was an expensive wait for the conniving jewelers, but they were willing to take the risk because the stakes were high. Meanwhile they plotted the robbery in detail. One of the jewelers had been a guest in the woman's home and was familiar with the layout of the place and the habits of the household.

On the day of the robbery he took the two hold-up men to the apartment house, waited until after the woman's husband had left for his office, and pointed out her apartment. He cautioned the gunmen to be sure to get the ring as it was her most important single piece of jewelry. Then he returned to his jewelry store two blocks away to await developments.

When the bandits walked into the store a short time later with the stolen jewelry, 47 pieces encrusted with 1200 diamonds, rubies and emeralds, the jeweler pretended to be greatly disappointed. "Where's the ring?" he demanded. "It's

177

the only thing I really wanted. This other stuff isn't worth much!" However, he said he would appraise the loot and settle with them next day. On the morrow he told them their haul was worth less than $25,000 and rather grudgingly gave them each $2500 in cash.

The two hoods departed for the East on the first plane, but no sooner had they arrived in their New York City hide-away than they saw newspaper stories stating the value of the jewelry at $175,000. This was a slight exaggeration, but even so the discrepancy between the jeweler's figure and the newspaper estimate was enough to make the gunmen extremely irritated. They promptly began working out a unique plan to extract their fair share from the jeweler. They contacted a known criminal in New York, a large, solidly built man who looked rather like a police officer, and outlined their scheme to him. He was to go to Beverly Hills, grab the jeweler, representing himself to be a policeman, and demand a $25,000 payoff from him to avoid arrest. He would then split this handsome fee with the gunmen.

It looked pretty good, but on thinking it over the bogus police officer was not enthusiastic about his chances of success. Furthermore, he faced a life sentence in New York State as a habitual criminal if he were caught making one more misstep. After considerable thought he made contact with us, offering to furnish information on the jewelry hold-up if we, in turn, would help him clear himself with New York authorities. We answered that if we could solve this vicious crime and recover the stolen property through his assistance we would notify the New York officials of his action, adding that they would probably consider it prime evidence of his sincere desire to rehabilitate himself.

Through his information we arrested the two stick-up men in New York City and the guilty jewelers in Beverly Hills, and recovered the missing jewelry. The jewels were returned by an attorney who reported that an unknown person had left a package in his office. He had opened the package, immediately recognized the jewels as stolen property, and

178

hurried to the police station with them. His explanation amused us since the jewelers at the time of their arrest had assured us that the gems would be returned by an intermediary.

During our investigation one of the hold-up men confessed that this same jeweler had employed him many years before to stage a fake robbery in his Los Angeles store to defraud an insurance company. He had been hired to hit the jeweler on the head, bind him, pick up loose jewelry and cash, and depart for New York. We looked up the old records and sure enough our friend the jeweler had been found, bound and gagged, in his shop with a small cut on his head, and had reported $80,000 worth of jewelry stolen. However, the missing gems had prudently been moved out of the store prior to the "robbery."

When I went to New York to bring back the two gunmen one of them had what he thought was an excellent alibi. He told me he had been at the Flamingo in Las Vegas at the time the jewel robbery was pulled. Bugsy Siegel had seen him there and could swear to it, he said. Two hours after I questioned him in New York police headquarters his attempted alibi went up in gunsmoke in Beverly Hills when a gangland executioner rubbed out Bugsy Siegel.

Frank Phillips, then a lieutenant in the New York main office squad, played a key role in apprehending our jewel robbers. Phillips and his officers set up two stake-outs to nab them, one in the Bronx and the other in Manhattan. The suspect in Manhattan, a narcotics user, was flushed out of a tenement house there by the narcotics squad. Both men were hardened criminals, and capturing them was dangerous business.

The guilty conspirators were convicted after a sensational trial in which Jerry Giesler represented one of the defendants and our present Municipal Judge, Adolph Alexander, then a deputy District Attorney, handled the prosecution. The two jewelers attacked the characters of their underworld confederates, protesting that we should not take the word of known criminals against "respectable" citizens. This usually happens in a major crime which involves one or more participants with police records; the others try to put the blame on the ex-convicts. It is obvious, however, that a person who wants a felony committed will pick a crook for the job rather than a pillar of society. He knows a criminal is capable of doing it.

We had a similar case recently in which a famous movie furrier conspired with two underworld characters to stage a fake robbery of his store in an attempt to defraud an insurance company. It began on a December night in 1955 when an ADT alarm summoned uniform officers and detectives to the city's leading fur emporium. When they arrived, the proprietor, Al Teitelbaum, showing marks of adhesive tape on his wrists and clothing, had a dramatic story to tell. Four bandits had forced their way into his store, bound him and an employee, and escaped with armloads of valuable furs.

The leader of the gang, he said, had entered his office at closing time, posing as an insurance adjuster, and conferred with him for almost an hour while the employees were leaving for the night. When only one employee, a fur cutter, was left in the store, the bandit had pulled a .45 caliber automatic from his brief case and ordered Teitelbaum to open the rear door, admitting three more men, two of them dressed in deliverymen's uniforms. These men also drew guns and forced Teitelbaum and the fur cutter to lie on the floor while they bound them with adhesive tape. The strangers then raided the fur racks and vault and departed. Later Teitelbaum and his companion worked themselves free and set off the alarm to summon police. A check of his stock revealed that 231 furs worth $248,000 were missing.

The police were interested in the furrier's story because he had been under observation on several previous occasions. A month earlier two supposed bandits had been routed when the janitor at the store saw them entering and set off the burglar alarm. Two years earlier Teitelbaum had reported a robbery under similar circumstances in which he said four bandits had made off with $125,000 worth of furs. A

Teitelbaum salesman-manager in a New York City hotel had also reported furs stolen from his rooms, but New York police found the missing furs in the hotel, one floor below, under suspicious circumstances. We had also received information that a known burglar had disposed of furs to Teitelbaum and that an ex-convict had sold furs for him on the outside with no receipts given.

Since 231 furs were claimed to be missing in this new robbery, we knew that a large vehicle would have been needed to carry them and considerable time required to load them. This large number of furs would have represented substantial bulk and weight. Our detectives canvassed the neighborhood for people who might have seen activity at the store, but could find no one who had seen any truck or other large conveyance in the vicinity at the time. Our patrol officer was convinced that there had been no unusual activity because he had passed the store at the time of the alleged robbery and had seen nothing. All officers on patrol near the fur store had previously been given instructions to be exceptionally alert in the vicinity of the store because of past robbery reports. This was the "hot spot" in town. We had also noticed that the furrier's ADT alarm had gone off numerous times previous to the robbery and wondered if this was to test the time required for police to arrive and to study our method of inspecting the premises.

Our investigation resulted in the apprehension of two ex-convicts who admitted they had been hired by Teitelbaum to stage a fake robbery for insurance purposes. They said he originally planned it a month earlier, but they had been frightened away when the janitor sounded the alarm. On their return engagement the janitor had conveniently been sent out of town and was unable to interrupt the proceedings.

The latest incident almost had a movie celebrity in it. The late Mario Lanza, the singing screen star, reported that he and his chauffeur had driven to the alley door of the store to pay a call on the furrier at 7 P.M. on the evening of the "robbery." When they got no answer after pounding on the rear door they went to the front of the store where they saw Teitelbaum and the fur-cutter inside and were admitted. The men told Lanza their story and showed him the tape marks on their wrists and clothing. He did not, however, see any truck or bandits.

At the trial which ended in his conviction, Teitelbaum received staunch support from many local business people, although he did not take the stand in his own defense. Long popular in the film colony for his custom of lending furs to movie stars and studios for publicity, he presented a list of character witnesses which read like a "Who's Who" of Hollywood: Joan Crawford, Dore Schary, Louella Parsons, Helen Rose and others. He was also supported by fur wholesalers who had supplied him with furs on consignment. Understandably, they wanted to see him vindicated so that he could collect the insurance money and pay them. I have learned to look behind the scenes at such trials and understand why certain people are interested in the welfare of the defendant.

Teitelbaum's conviction was just the beginning of his case. He fought the indictment with every possible legal maneuver for more than three years, taking 25 different legal actions before he finally started his one-year sentence in County Jail on August, 1959. He stoutly protested his innocence as the jail doors clanged behind him and complained he had been convicted on the testimony of reprehensible individuals with police records. Several prominent citizens wrote to the Governor in his behalf, praising him as a fine fellow.

Like the jewel robbery which preceded it, the Teitelbaum case revealed a surprise solution for a crime which had occurred years earlier. During our investigation, a retired safe-cracker, now an elderly man in poor health, reported to us that he had been hired by the furrier's father more than 30 years before to fake a burglary of the fur vault in his Chicago store. The elder Teitelbaum, now deceased, recruited the safe-cracker to break into the vault on a week-end, telling him that an envelope containing $2000 in greenbacks would be waiting for him inside the vault. The man worked all Saturday night and into Sunday morning getting the door open, but when he opened the envelope it held only $500. Since he was in no position to complain to the Chicago police, the safe-cracker said nothing, but he carried a grudge for the rest of his life and told us about it when he thought his end was near.

At the Teitelbaum trial, television on-the-scene reporting was introduced into the courtroom for the first time. After the furrier's arrest, television cameras set up by newscasters at police headquarters had filmed an interview with me. The defense attorney subpoenaed the film and the cameraman projected it for the court and jury during the trial, marking a new use for television.

It was interesting to note that in both the jewel and the fur robbery cases the defendants had no trouble producing reliable citizens as character witnesses. People often step forward as witnesses for felons because they sincerely believe them to be nice fellows. Most crooks lead a Dr. Jekyll-and-Mr. Hyde existence. They show only their good side to the public, but to the police they will always be evil Mr. Hydes.

twenty

GOLD PLATED

DELINQUENTS

JUVENILE DELINQUENCY IS PROBABLY THE MOST IMPOR-
tant law enforcement problem in America today. Among the
various theories sociologists and others have advanced, I dis-
agree with the argument that eradication of underprivileged
conditions and the possession of the good things in life is a
cure-all for crime. This has not proved true in my police experience in Beverly Hills where youngsters in trouble are
almost without exception, over privileged. Although we have
one of the lowest ratios of juvenile delinquency per capita
in the United States, the number of local youths who get in
trouble with the law every year indicates that fine homes,
swimming pools, wads of spending money and automobiles
do not solve the problem.

Wealth is as likely to cause delinquency as to cure it. I
have seen youngsters who had everything money could buy
become as dangerously delinquent as the poorest kid in any
big city slum. Often this is because they have too much money

184

and too little to do. Some have the problem of being famous because of their parents and find it impossible to adjust to normal living. Their widely-publicized misdemeanors reflect unfavorably on the community. I have known older delinquents who squandered their parents' wealth and became derelicts, several of them ending in State prisons.

Two sons of well-known actors living in Beverly Hills have been nothing but trouble for many years although they were given every advantage by their parents. The son of a prominent motion-picture agent cost his father thousands of dollars by his habit of writing bad checks, from grammar-school age to maturity. Others have committed crimes for thrills, like the wealthy merchant's son who burglarized homes in his neighborhood "just for kicks," and the three teen-agers who pilfered their own homes while their parents were out of town. One 14-year-old boy from a good family broke into so many residences that we thought a crime wave was upon us until we set detectives to watch the area and caught him.

We nabbed another high-school boy who was a party raider. He would slip out of his bedroom at night and roam the neighborhood looking for signs of social activity. When he found a house where a party was in progress he would sneak to the rear of the residence, enter by a door or window, and empty the ladies' handbags in the guest room. By the time the loss was discovered he would be safely in bed at home. His parents were unaware of his thievery because he always went to bed early, then dressed and climbed out of his window.

The 17-year-old son of a prosperous contractor held up a victim at gunpoint and robbed him on a dare. Quickly captured, he was sent to reform school where he met other youths who used narcotics and became a user himself. Later he used his father's credit cards to buy new tires and sold them in order to get money to supply his dope habit. Within a few years he was in prison, serving a term for armed robbery and burglary. His chances of rehabilitation are slim, as are those of a 16-year-old boy who began associating with narcotics users in Los Angeles and became an addict himself.

I remember the son of a wealthy oil man who repeatedly grieved his family by passing bad checks which his father made good. After his father's death he squandered what was left of the family fortune. The last time I saw him he was doing time as a trusty in a small county jail in Central California. Another rich young man used to turn in false fire alarms just for the thrill of seeing and hearing fire engines converging on him. His problem was a sex aberration as well as too much money.

One warm night a Beverly Hills couple who had been sitting in a parked car reported to the police with some astonishment that a completely nude man had run across the street in front of them. Since no one else in the vicinity had seen this unusual spectacle we assumed our informants had imagined it. A few nights later, however, a woman in an apartment house called to report that a nude man had peered in her bedroom window. As a patrol car quietly approached the apartment house by way of an alley the officers were surprised to see the naked figure of a young man leap out into the glare of the headlights. He was captured after a short chase and found to be a mentally-retarded teen-ager who had been making a nightly custom of prowling alleys in the nude and spying on women.

Another "peeping Tom" whom we caught repeatedly outside the windows of Beverly Hills homes after dark was the teen-age son of a lawyer. Instead of cooperating with the police in controlling the boy, the father defended him vigorously each time he was arrested. Later the family moved to another city where the youth became an active, aggressive sex criminal. I have always felt that this sad ending could have been avoided if the boy's father had listened to our advice instead of fighting us.

Parents often contribute unwittingly to the delinquency of their children by refusing to cooperate with the police

186

department after their offspring have been picked up for minor offenses. Recently two teen-age boys from fine homes in Beverly Hills were arrested as "Lover's Lane" bandits. Armed with guns and flashlights they went up to Mulholland Drive, a scenic mountain highway behind our city much favored by romantic couples, and held up "petting parties." I blamed the parents as much as the boys for what happened. Earlier we had had both boys and their parents at headquarters and had asked the parents to cooperate with us in disciplinary and supervisory measures for the boys' welfare. However, the parents took a hostile and defensive attitude which only encouraged their sons to defy the police more openly next time, to their ultimate sorrow.

Teen-age offenders frequently have expensive tastes in Beverly Hills. One youth became delinquent because he felt underprivileged when his parents would not replace his 1956 Thunderbird with a later model. We had two other youngsters who stole an expensive sports car for a joy ride to Las Vegas, and a 15-year-old girl who was picked up doing 80 miles an hour in a Mercedes 300 SL.

I remember one teen-age girl who resorted to shoplifting when her once wealthy parents could no longer afford a high scale of living. The family moved into a modest apartment so that the girl could continue as a student at Beverly Hills High School, but in order to get a suitable wardrobe she stole from the expensive shops where her parents formerly had charge accounts. She explained her new clothes to her mother as gifts from girl friends. Before we caught up with her she lifted $1000 worth of wearing apparel.

A wealthy girl who had everything was in love with a boy from a broken home. One night she wanted to go dancing at the Cocoanut Grove in Los Angeles, but the boy had no automobile. She solved this problem by persuading him to take one of the four cars owned by her next-door neighbor. When they returned from their date five hours later the police were waiting and took the boy into custody for automobile theft. He was sent to a juvenile detention camp, but the ties of love were stronger than the law and he escaped three times. Each time he was found hiding in the same place, the unoccupied servants' quarters in the rear of his sweetheart's Beverly Hills estate. This romance should have had a happy ending, but I believe the young lady later fell in love with a young man who had an automobile of his own.

Juveniles have always tended to be delinquent, as youth always rebels against authority, but only in recent years has so much attention been paid to them. We are faced with conditions that were not present two generations ago when our grandparents had to work 12 hours a day, not because they liked it but because it was necessary for survival. Today the emphasis in our culture is on freedom. Nothing must interfere with individual self-expression from the cradle to the grave. Parents seek to spare their children from the difficulties they encountered by providing extra comforts for them, thus robbing them of individual responsibility.

Wise parents—and there are many of them in Beverly Hills—make their children earn possessions and privileges. No youngster should have things too easy. Teen-agers do not have to have automobiles as a natural right. Millions of people have to walk every day, and are probably healthier for it.

In earlier days, parents did not let their children go to the movies until they themselves had screened them. There is little such supervision today and the kids can turn on the television set in the living-room to scenes of violence and delinquency. Lack of individual discipline and moral responsibility are basic causes of the problem. To prevent delinquency parents must know what their children are doing, whom they are associating with, and how late they stay out. The later the hour, the more likely the youngsters are to get into trouble.

Sometimes socially ambitious families demand too much from their offspring. The children may be equipped only to be ordinary citizens, but their parents try to force them into responsibilities they cannot handle. I know of one wealthy doctor's son who rejected his parents' ambitious plans for him and is now doing well as a mechanic and garage owner.

Juvenile delinquency in Beverly Hills is not attributable to any lack of parental interest in the situation. Many of our leading citizens and celebrities, like proud parents everywhere, are active in church work, Boy Scouts, Girl Scouts, Little League, YMCA and other character-forming organizations. Among the local residents who devote their time to youth work are motion-picture and television stars like James Stewart, Robert Young, Danny Thomas, Glenn Ford and Eleanor Powell, to name a few.

Through the years I have watched the careers of graduates of Beverly Hills High School, many of them now civic and industrial leaders. Only a very small percentage of them ever went astray, and some of them were irresponsible kids whom we salvaged and rehabilitated. One former high school student, whom we once arrested for stealing automobiles, is now the president of a local company and a highly respected citizen.

Playgrounds and recreational facilities have their place in combatting delinquency, but supervised play is not enough. Youngsters need something to do which makes them feel important and gives them a sense of achievement. Otherwise they will lose interest and seek more exciting outlets for their energy.

Modern methods of handling young delinquents may not be as effective as our old-style ways. Years ago when we picked up an errant youth we would take his problem up immediately and directly with his parents, the school authorities and his church. Today we have become so scientific that every case is likely to become a project for social workers, psychologists and other experts. I would like to see more authority given to teachers and school officials in handling juvenile delinquents, instead of pampering them at Juvenile Hall and turning them over to psychiatrists. I have observed that medical and mental treatments rarely work unless the patient sincerely wants to be cured.

I remember the case of the psychiatrist and the car thief. For several weeks we were puzzled by the activity of a bold thief who stole automobiles with clocklike regularity. He always hit on Wednesday afternoons and always in the same neighborhood. Close by on the following day we would find an abandoned car which had been reported stolen in the Hollywood area. After three weeks of this illegal automobile trading we covered the area with detectives on a Wednesday afternoon and awaited developments.

One of the detectives saw a teen-age youth park a car on the street and walk into the building where many doctors had their offices. Ordinarily he would have paid no attention to the boy, but because of the circumstances he decided to watch him. An hour or so later the boy came out of the building and the detective tailed him. Sure enough, the youth ignored the car he had left by the curb and sauntered into a nearby parking lot where he began checking for automobiles that had ignition keys in the locks. He found a well-appointed Lincoln he liked and was driving away in it when we nabbed him.

We discovered that the young culprit had been arrested frequently for auto theft in Los Angeles and was currently in care of the Probation Department. As part of his rehabilitation he had been ordered to undergo psychiatric treatment. His parents sent him to a well-known psychiatrist in Beverly Hills in order to get the best possible treatment for him. Every Wednesday after school he would methodically steal a car and drive to our city for his appointment with the doctor, and on leaving the psychiatric couch would steal another car for the trip home. Apparently the young man just liked to steal cars and no treatment could cure him. He was later sent to a forestry camp where there were no automobiles and this disciplinary action had a salutary effect on him.

In our work with juveniles, we are as much concerned with protecting the innocent as apprehending the guilty. Children of wealthy families are subject to many dangers and we are constantly on the alert to guard them from unscrupulous individuals. One young actress, formerly a child movie star, was almost the victim of an older man with a police record, who plotted to get her to run away with him. A friend of the girl notified me that the man was meeting the girl daily in a city park without the knowledge of her family. I immediately called a family conference and revealed to the starlet and her parents the record of this middle-aged Lothario. Later I called the man into my office for a quiet talk. He had done nothing for which I could arrest him at this point, but he departed and annoyed the girl no more after he found we were wise to his scheme.

When young Pia Bergman suddenly became the frightened target of public interest in 1950 after her famous mother, Ingrid Bergman, eloped with an Italian motion-picture director, the girl's grammar-school principal requested police cooperation in protecting the child from curiosity seekers. The principal felt that the girl should be permitted to lead a normal life and continue her school work unmolested. We took steps to make this possible. It is one of our regular police duties to protect Beverly Hills schoolgrounds, particularly when youngsters going to and coming from school might be exposed to questionable contacts.

We have to be always on the alert to shield citizens, young and old, from blackmail and extortion, and keep a sharp lookout for unprincipled men and women. Sometimes we find evil in unexpected places, such as designing mothers who seek to get their daughters intimately involved with wealthy men for financial gain.

We have been fortunate in our city in having the cooperation of school officials, churches and civic groups in combatting juvenile delinquency, and this is essential because the police cannot do it alone. Every student in our public schools is given a copy of a guidebook entitled "Laws for Youth," which is prepared by the police department, the Parent-Teachers Association and service clubs. This booklet states the basic principles of conduct for youth and warns them of possible dangers. We frequently get requests for it from other cities and organizations.

Because of the wealth in Beverly Hills, we watch youth group activities closely to keep dubious characters from becoming associated with them. I remember one confidence man, a bad-check artist, who suddenly became active in a youth organization in a local church. When the church leaders asked me about him I told them what I knew. The con man shortly afterward dropped out of the group. He was found to be less interested in religion than in meeting a girl with money. We never try to keep anyone away from church who is sincerely interested in the finer things of life, but if he is there for a sinister purpose we can easily detect it. Experienced police officers know genuine reform when they see it, and con men seldom mend their ways.

twenty-one

CITY OF

BROKEN DREAMS

HOLLYWOOD OFFERS THE WORLD ON A STRING TO SOME, but to others a passport to tragedy. During my years as a Beverly Hills policeman I have seen men and women who once were prominent in the motion-picture colony become derelicts. In their race to gain fame and fortune, they forgot the most important thing about living, which is to live right. I have also known business men who spent years acquiring millions only to end it all by suicide. Money did not bring them happiness.

We used to pick up and jail a high-salaried film producer who lost his family, friends and reputation when he became a chronic drunk, and I once had to arrest the late Marshall "Mickey" Neilan on bad check charges. When I first knew this noted motion-picture director he was earning $4000 a week and was one of the most popular men socially in Beverly Hills.

Fame was also cruel to Helen Lee Worthing. A statuesque Ziegfeld Follies beauty of the 1920s, she was judged by

Harrison Fisher, the artist, to have the most beautiful profile in America and selected by Mary Pickford as one of the three prettiest girls in the nation. Summoned to Hollywood for what promised to be a brilliant screen career, she appeared in pictures with John Barrymore and Adolphe Menjou. However, her beauty was not equaled by her ability as an actress and her star faded rapidly. As the months of waiting for more screen roles went by, Miss Worthing put up a gay front at Hollywood parties and began increasingly to rely on alcohol to buoy up her courage. But no more calls came from the studios for her services and pretty soon the party invitations stopped too. As her dream of greatness vanished the unfortunate young beauty drank herself into forgetfulness. In a short time she became a common drunk and, later, a narcotics addict.

For the next 20 years Helen Lee Worthing was a pathetic police case in Los Angeles and Hollywood. She was picked up drunk on the street, jailed after a drunken brawl with a man in a cheap lodging-house, arrested for narcotics violations several times, treated for cuts and bruises sustained in a fight with a "boy friend" on Skid Row, and once was put in the County "psycho" ward on an insanity complaint.

When she died in 1948, she was living in a three-room shack on a back lot in Hollywood which she shared with a Filipino houseman who had been her only friend for years. Hollywood had quickly forgotten her, but she had not forgotten her dream. Thick scrapbooks bulging with articles praising her beauty were at her bedside when she died, a victim of barbiturate poisoning. The final tally in her life record was made by the Public Administrator who put a total value on her worldly goods of $16.80.

This has been a city of broken dreams for many people who have been lured here to seek the pot of gold at the foot of Hollywood's rainbow. We have pretty girls working as waitresses in Beverly Hills who arrived in Hollywood as beauty contest winners with high hopes of becoming actresses. They soon discovered that beautiful women are plentiful here,

194

but only a talented few ever make the grade as actresses. Too proud to go back home defeated, they stay on to work at any jobs they can find.

One handsome young man from a wealthy Eastern family left his wife and children behind and came to Hollywood to be an actor. When no studio opened its gates to him, and his money ran short, he began associating with an ex-convict and finally landed in Beverly Hills jail as a hold-up man. A pretty television actress passed $1000 in worthless checks in order to maintain herself in a fashionable apartment while waiting for work. When we arrested her she claimed that a wealthy business man had promised to marry her and would make good on her checks. We released her on this story, but she skipped to Oklahoma City where she was re-arrested. The business man never materialized.

I have known ambitious mothers, with daughters they want to get in the movies, who have resorted to writing bad checks when they ran out of funds after months of waiting for studio auditions. One mother, whose daughter finally succeeded in becoming a teen-age star, was arrested half a dozen times for passing bad checks. I doubt if the girl's short screen career was worth the unhappiness it caused her family. Other mothers have been victimized by "talent school" promoters who promised them movie jobs for their children.

Movie-struck teen-agers sometimes run away from home in other sections of the United States and come to Beverly Hills. Two young runaways once hid out in Harold Lloyd's large estate, spending the nights rolled up on his garden furniture. A leading actor arrived home with his wife one night to find a teen-age girl asleep on his living-room couch. We put her up for the night in the juvenile section of the jail and sent her home. The recent popularity of television "westerns" has brought us a new kind of runaways, young fellows in cowboy outfits who want to meet their favorite he-man stars. These we hold until their parents arrive or send for them, and they go home disappointed.

I have seen dreams of happy marriage broken in Beverly

Hills many times. Couples who live normal married lives in sheltered circumstances elsewhere in the United States and Europe come here and are carried away by the glamour of the entertainment world. Frequently one member of the couple becomes infatuated with the social life of the film colony and their marriage goes on the rocks. It happened recently in the home of a noted song writer from the Midwest whose wife of many years' standing became a gay social figure and is now a gay divorcee.

Buster Keaton stated the local marital problem simply many years ago when he was divorced by Natalie Talmadge. At the time he was one of the great slapstick comedians of the screen. He had earned a fortune from his acting and lived it up in a $200,000 Italian-style mansion on an estate adjoining the Tom Mix place. At the time of the divorce he said, sadly, "We can't be happy here—we ought to be on a farm!" Later Buster went broke, but he survived financial disaster and made a praiseworthy comeback in television.

Wealth is no panacea for unhappy people. Under stress and strain some individuals cannot take it, regardless of their riches. Their problems are to them just as insurmountable as those of less fortunate human beings. And in some cases, they try suicide as a way out. One Beverly Hills citizen killed himself rather than go to court on a drunk-driving charge after his car had knocked over a fire plug. Most people would have faced up to the charge.

Late one night while I was patrolling a side street near the Los Angeles Country Club, I found a man lying on the ground moaning, covered with blood from a bullet wound in his head. Since I could find no weapon near him in the darkness, I assumed he had been shot by an unknown assailant and dumped from an automobile. The man died at the emergency hospital a short time later, where investigation revealed that his wound was self-inflicted. He had committed suicide rather than face the consequences of a criminal offense. At daybreak I returned to the spot where I had found him and traced a trail of blood to a tree 200 feet away, where he had shot himself and dropped the gun. Apparently he had changed his mind about wanting to die and had crawled all that distance mortally wounded, a remarkable physical feat.

People who are disappointed in love, or despondent over domestic troubles or financial woes, frequently make half-hearted attempts at suicide in a bid for sympathy. We have often been called to pick up unconscious individuals who, on being revived, claim they have taken handfuls of sleeping pills in order to bring about a reconciliation after a lover's quarrel. Many successful suicides are accidents. The victims did not really want to die, but yearned for sympathy and understanding. I have always felt that Lupe Velez, the lively Mexican movie star, never really intended to kill herself when she ended her life at the age of 34 with an overdose of sleeping pills. We found her dead in bed in her home, with a suicide note beside her addressed to her lover in which she wrote brokenly of unrequited love and expectant motherhood. I believe Lupe thought her act would bring her faithless lover back, but she miscalculated the amount of sleeping pills.

One famous football star shot himself after a quarrel with his girl friend and telephoned her to report his attempted suicide. We doubted the seriousness of his intentions, however, because the bullet only creased his buttocks. Another man, a prominent manufacturer, shot himself in the toe in what was supposed to be a suicide try. He was having domestic difficulties at the time.

Although the majority of our citizens are temperate, Beverly Hills has, I'm afraid, problem drinkers and we have investigated many tragic situations in which individuals have resorted to drink to escape loneliness. Psychiatrists say that most alcoholism is caused by loneliness, and I have found that people in Beverly Hills mansions can get just as lonely as the "winos" on Skid Row in other cities. I have known a half-dozen wealthy individuals who died of acute alcoholism without their condition ever becoming known to the public. There was, for instance, an heir to a grocery-store fortune who died in a mansion attended by a maid, butler and other

197

domestics. Never a derelict, never seen on the street drunk, he drank himself to death surrounded by luxury.

One wealthy bachelor with a weakness for liquor lived alone in a large house on a canyon estate in Beverly Hills. He proved to be an easy target for an unscrupulous group of drinking companions with a craving for money. These pals moved in and kept him drunk for days at a time. Meanwhile they conned him into writing personal checks which they speedily cashed at a Santa Monica bank, pocketing the proceeds themselves. After this had gone on for several weeks the bank became suspicious of the number of checks the wealthy drunk was writing and asked us to investigate. We paid a call to his mansion and arrested his guests on charges of conspiracy to commit grand theft.

Everybody wants to be noticed and appreciated by his fellow men, and some individuals are willing to break the law and undergo unhappiness just to have a little bit of personal fame. One such was the 23-year-old son of a Beverly Hills domestic who was an avid reader of detective stories. He was a quiet, introverted fellow who lived with his mother in the servants' quarters of a large estate. Nobody paid much attention to him, but secretly he had dreams of glory. One night he set out to prove himself. He stole the automobile of his mother's employer and held up two theaters, the Warner Brothers theater in Beverly Hills and Grauman's Chinese Theater in Hollywood. When a parking lot attendant at the Chinese Theater tried to prevent him from driving away in another stolen car he shot the man, but did not wound him seriously.

After the shooting he became a fugitive and roamed hobo jungles all over the United States. Wherever he went on the bum he heard the old-timers telling of their past scrapes with the police. Not to be outdone, he began boasting of his prowess as a hold-up man and embroidered his story with the declaration that he had killed a man. But nobody would believe him. Unable to stand their disbelief he finally turned

198

himself in at the Santa Monica police station, simply to prove his claim to fame.

The Santa Monica police wouldn't believe him either and the desk officer called me to ask about him. "Say, I've got some screwball here who says he pulled a couple of hold-ups and killed a man," he said. "Do you know anything about him." We looked up the record and found that he hadn't murdered anyone but had held up the theaters. This dreamer of broken dreams was put away in County Jail to ponder his record and in time, no doubt, he got over his embarrassment at not being a killer.

twenty-two

TELLERS

OF TALES

FALSE REPORTS OF ROBBERY, BURGLARY, KIDNAPPING, assault and other crimes are an old story to policemen everywhere. In times of stress, ordinary citizens can come up with some remarkably imaginative tales. Since veteran officers can quickly detect bogus reports, and have heard every variety, I often wonder why people keep on trying to fool the police.

We had one local houseman who called headquarters to report a burglary. Patrol officers arrived at the scene to find the house looking like a small cyclone had struck it. The screen door was pushed inside out, and the living-room littered with broken dishes and splintered furniture. The houseman, showing scars of battle, told a dramatic story. He had been alone in the house during the absence of the owners. Two burglars had broken in shortly before dawn, and he had leaped to the defense of his employer's property, fighting them off after a terrific struggle.

The physical evidence seemed to support his account, except that the screen door, through which he said the intruders had entered, was damaged only on the inside. After considerable questioning the houseman finally blurted out the truth. He had been entertaining a girl friend and, unfortunately, she had become belligerent. She had thrown dishes at him and broken chairs in wild swings at his head. In the scuffle to remove her from the premises other furniture had been damaged. When he surveyed the wreckage in the cold light of morning, with the return of his employers imminent, the only alibi he could dream up was the burglary yarn. It was a good try.

Another touching story came from a fellow who had promised to marry a Beverly Hills girl. A date had been set for the wedding. But just before the happy day arrived he reported to police that he had been kidnapped and robbed by unidentified strangers who had taken all his money. Under the circumstances he felt it would be impossible for him to go through with the wedding. The nuptials were called off, but our investigation proved his robbery report false. The truth was that he already had a wife and got cold feet on the eve of what would have been a bigamous marriage.

A well-known tennis star was found in a dazed condition here sporting a black eye and a bloody shirt. Since there was some publicity incident to his arrest, the tennis player tried to justify himself in the newspapers by concocting a story of police brutality. His wretched appearance was the work of police officers, he said, who had arrested him without cause and roughed him up when he objected. What had really happened was that he and a companion had engaged in a street brawl from which he emerged second best.

Many times people arrested for drunkenness or disorderly conduct will deny it the morning after, and blame "police brutality" for their predicament in a bid for public sympathy. The human thing, of course, is to believe a fellow-citizen's story that he has been victimized by the police. In Beverly Hills, because of the prominence of our "clientele" and the tendency of news media to play up datelines from our city, we are always sure of our facts before we make an arrest.

On a December afternoon in 1954 the switchboard at police headquarters lit up like a Christmas tree with calls from citizens reporting a series of hit-and-run traffic crashes in the 400 and 600 blocks on North Camden Drive. Officers in patrol cars converged on the area and found the actress Marie MacDonald, once famous as "The Body," at the wheel of her Cadillac. It had collided with a smaller sedan after hitting several parked cars.

Miss MacDonald appeared to be dazed, and was taken to the Receiving Hospital in an ambulance. An examination by the doctor on duty revealed that she had been taking nembutal pills and seconal sedatives. She was extremely belligerent. It took the combined efforts of two officers and a policewoman to put her in a cell. Later the jailer heard glass breaking and discovered that Miss MacDonald had taken off her shoe and broken the glass in the light-well with her heel.

Two additional officers and the policewoman joined forces to move her into another cell. In the process she kicked one officer in the groin and bit the other on the hand. This time they took away her shoes to protect the cell light from damage. A short time later her husband, Harry Karl, and a physician arrived, as well as her mother and Attorney Lloyd Wright, Jr. The physician prescribed pills for a pain in her stomach. The attorney contacted Municipal Judge Draeger and requested her release, assuring the judge that the actress would be kept under constant nursing care. She was released on her own recognizance.

Meanwhile the commotion had attracted the interest of the newspapers, and a group of reporters and photographers waited for Miss MacDonald outside the jail. As she was being released she again became unruly. Her husband, trying to be a knight in armor, attempted to stave off photographers. He put the actress in his car and made such a fast getaway that the car knocked a camera out of a newsman's hand and almost ran down another photographer. (Later the photographer filed a complaint with the District Attorney charging assault with a deadly weapon. This charge was subsequently reduced, and Mr. Karl was fined $500.)

At her hearing, Miss MacDonald was represented by Jerry Giesler and others, who convinced the court that she was a sick person in need of medical treatment and not a criminal. She was allowed to plead guilty to a lesser offense. At this time the police department did not object to the light treatment accorded the actress because of representations which had been made that she was a sick woman. Apologies had been extended for her unladylike conduct and restitution made for all damages.

This closed the chapter on the MacDonald case as far as the police department was concerned. Everyone involved felt nothing but sympathy for the actress, and the disagreeable incident had been forgotten. We were considerably surprised, therefore, a short time later when the wire services released a news story from Honolulu in which Miss MacDonald charged our department with brutality. Among other things, she was quoted as saying our officers had kicked her in the stomach! There was not one kind word about the consideration shown her. The sad fact in such an untrue and unfavorable attack on a fine police department is that there are always people who are ready to believe it.

Because of our proximity to Hollywood, we view with suspicion news stories on arrests where publicity agents are concerned. Depending on an actor's need for publicity, a simple little argument between two friends can be blown up into a full-fledged fight.

A handsome male star who had not been getting enough publicity to satisfy him was once the subject of a news item which aroused my official interest. I read in a metropolitan newspaper that the star had been held up by a man with a gun in his room at a prominent Beverly Hills hotel. The story went on to say that just as the gunman was about to make off with the actor's money and valuables the actor had begged him not to take a memento of his military service in World

War II, which he carried as a keepsake. The robber had looked closely at the keepsake and almost burst into tears. "My God! I didn't recognize you," he exclaimed. "You and I were in the same outfit!" The gunman begged the star's forgiveness, returned his money and hurried away.

Since there had been no police report of this robbery attempt, I hastened to the hotel to investigate. I found the star in his room, and listened to his story. He said the gunman had entered the room about 6 A.M., an hour in which I knew the room would have been too dark for anyone to be recognized. "How did he recognize you in the dark?" I inquired. While the actor was thinking of an answer I glanced through an open bedroom door and saw an attractive blonde who apparently was there as his guest. At this I advised the star that the presence of a girl in his rooms might possibly be a violation of our innkeeper's ordinance, and suggested that he tell me the truth, unless he wanted to be the subject of further investigation.

The actor quickly admitted that his story was a hoax. His career had been in the doldrums since his return to Hollywood, he said. He hadn't been getting any work and he just wanted to get his name before the public again.

Amateur gamblers, and husbands who lose their wives' house money betting on the races, frequently try to solve their financial dilemmas by reporting false hold-ups. We had one Beverly Hills husband who had gambled and lost heavily at a desert resort. He had promised to pay his losses at a certain date, but when the time came he didn't have the money, and the gamblers, who are expert collection men, were on his trail. He reported he had been held up and robbed of exactly the amount he owed the gamblers. His story, to no one's surprise, proved to be phoney.

Wives also try the same dodge, though less frequently. I remember two who reported their fur coats stolen, valued at $5000. We traced the coats and discovered that the wives had paid off their losses to a bookie with them, and had concocted the theft story to keep their husbands from knowing. We enjoy particularly close cooperation from insurance company operatives and private detectives in checking out crime reports. Since more people here carry heavy insurance against theft than in an average city, thefts are more likely to be reported to the police.

Even bookmakers have unwittingly been victims of betting fever, like the bookie whose wife took his money out of a safety-deposit box and lost it on the races without telling him. When this shortage forced him to welsh on some bets, his wife tried a fake kidnapping as a cover-up. She reported to police that her small son had been kidnapped by a man who had taken her to the bank and forced her to remove $30,000 ransom money from the safety-deposit box. Her story sounded plausible enough, but when we asked the little boy to describe the kidnapper for us he piped up: "The man was a friend of Mamma's!"

Although police can't always prove a bogus hold-up report, sometimes circumstances offer a solution. We had one employee in a local laundry office who claimed he was held up and robbed of company cash while on duty. His story wasn't convincing. We traced his background and found he had been robbed under identical circumstances in an eastern state. We confronted him with the facts and he quit the company. This was 20 years ago, and the laundry hasn't had another hold-up since.

Mysterious telephone calls demanding money or making threats are not always as sinister as they seem. Sometimes they are from members of the victim's family—children trying to intimidate parents, a husband or wife attempting to throw a scare into the other partner. When Stan Laurel, the much-married English comedian, lived in Beverly Hills he was plagued by a series of anonymous phone calls and complained to the police. We discovered the calls were coming from his wife, jealous over the attention he was showing one of his ex-wives.

On one occasion our police were hoaxed unintentionally. We had an ambulance call to "restaurant row," a street noted for its many fine eating places. We found a well-dressed man lying on the parkway outside a restaurant, moaning and groaning, with sweat pouring out of him. He had been stricken with a pain in his chest while eating, and was almost scared to death. His best friend, he gasped, had recently had a heart attack just like this.

We took him to the Receiving Hospital where a doctor examined him but found nothing wrong. After he calmed down he walked out of the hospital a new man. He was mistaken in his fear, but the police were ready to believe him. It has been our experience through the years that a surprising number of people die from overeating and overdrinking, even in the fine restaurants of Beverly Hills.

Fake suicides with sleeping pills are an occasional problem here as in other cities. Usually the subjects are trying to get attention, or sympathy, or win back the affection of a straying sweetheart. Our ambulance drivers have picked up enough "suicides" to know a fake when they see it. They have a sure cure for such hoaxes: A quick trip to the emergency hospital where the "victim's" stomach is pumped out. I can't remember of any suicide faker coming in for a second pumping!

Frequently the police are pictured as villains because of misinformation given to news media. Our "Betsy Ross" incident was a case in point. We found a woman conducting a dressmaking business in an apartment house located in a residential zone. She had converted a double apartment into a little factory and salesroom; fitting room in front and work room in the rear. When other occupants of the house complained that the noise of the sewing machine was disturbing them, police investigated and rightfully ordered the dressmaker to move her activities into a commercial zone.

One of the dressmaker's customers was the wife of a newspaper man, and reported to her husband that the seamstress was being unjustly used. She averred that the woman was making American Flags for the Veterans' Home at Sawtelle when the police stopped her. The husband, naturally,

206

wrote his wife's version of the story with all stops pulled out. It appeared in a metropolitan newspaper under a headline accusing the Beverly Hills police of persecuting a "Betsy Ross," a highly unpatriotic act—and just when she was sewing Flags for veterans, too! Nevertheless, like Washington at Valley Forge, we stood fast in our unpopular but necessary position, and the dressmaker moved her business into a commercial zone where it belonged.

Frequently people financially interested in motion pictures which are exhibited without the official seal of purity telephone me to express their deep concern for the protection of the morals of the community. They then ask me if I am not going to ban a certain picture when it reaches Beverly Hills. My answer is that I am not interested in their problem. What they are trying to do is to use the police department to gain publicity.

Whenever a big case breaks, with wealthy and prominent people involved, we are deluged with publicity seekers who want to get into the act. Astrologers, numerologists, palmists and would-be detectives all come forward with suggestions. To date I can't remember one of them ever solving anything. We had one woman who claimed to be a spiritualist with accurate information from the "other world" about a jewelry robbery which she wanted to pass along to the victim. As usual, her tip was worthless.

A red-haired divorcee from Georgia caused us more trouble than any other one woman I can remember. She was an attractive woman in her thirties, apparently cultured, who had married into a wealthy and prominent Southern family and was living comfortably in Beverly Hills.

At first she was just a voice on the telephone at headquarters, inquiring in accents which dripped with honey and magnolias: "Can't a poor woman from the South get any protection from all the wolves here?" And she went on to complain that different men had been annoying her.

Frequently persons who are planning some illegal activity will telephone the police department first to test the gullibility of its personnel. We soon discovered that the woman from Georgia was one of this type. But she did not find us gullible.

On her first visit to the office she requested the arrest of her daughter for absconding with $1600. After checking her story we told her she did not have a bonafide complaint, and she went away unhappy.

Her next appearance was at the City Prosecutor's office to get a complaint filed against a prominent doctor for hit-run driving. She charged that his car had brushed against her at an intersection, injuring her. She was referred to the police department, but since we had knowledge of her activities we were suspicious that her report was another phoney. We advised her we would not file a complaint without witnesses or physical evidence.

Three days later she brought in a young fellow who said he had seen the accident, but it was obvious he had been coached. He worked as a soda jerk in a drug store at the intersection in question. Later detectives interviewed him alone. He admitted that the divorcee had promised him $20 if he would be her witness. She had told him she was going to take the doctor for $15,000 or $20,000 damages and would give him a share of it.

We arranged for the young man to telephone the divorcee from the police station, with a detective listening in on the line, and tell her he was worried about their deal. She laughed off his doubts. "You don't have to worry about the dumb cops," she said as we listened in. "I've outsmarted them and the insurance companies many times." This hit-and-run case was just peanuts, she told him. She had much bigger things in mind.

She described her great idea for collecting money from department stores by fake shoplifting. She would carry silver candlesticks from her home into stores, with receipts showing they had been paid for and were her property, and would loiter near store counters and let clerks see the candlesticks under her coat. When they called the store detectives she would sue for false arrest.

She had been making a good living for years by such schemes, she told him. In one case she had received $500 each from a drug store and a manufacturer by threatening to sue them for selling her faulty medicine. They all would rather pay off a nuisance claim than go to court, she explained. In conclusion, she told the fellow that if he needed money she would give him $100 right now.

We promptly arrested the Georgia redhead for soliciting perjury. She was convicted after a jury trial, then turned on her lawyer and accused him of improper conduct, and also raised the familiar charge of "police persecution." She tried to enlist the sympathies of other lawyers, civic and fraternal organizations, and stirred up the American Civil Liberties Union in her behalf. Despite her efforts she was sentenced to County Jail, and later released on probation on condition that she return to Georgia.

Among other local residents who were happy to see her go were two apartment-house landlords who had been her favorite pigeons. She had collected $1000 from one by threatening him with an OPA rent control complaint, and $1500 from the other. The latter, an elderly man, answered her call to fix the bathroom shower in her apartment. Later she charged he had caused her untold humiliation by "invading" the bathroom while her scantily-clad daughter was in it. She threatened suit and he settled out of court, although our investigation showed he was innocent of any wrongdoing.

Surprisingly enough, at the trial of the Georgia divorcee several respectable citizens took the stand as witnesses to her good character. Over the years I have found that smart confidence operators, particularly women, can fool laymen most of the time, and sometimes even judges and juries. Policemen, however, have to be more skeptical about their fellowmen.

twenty-three

GOOD POLICEMEN

ARE BORN

IF YOU HAVE BEEN WATCHING TELEVISION DRAMAS lately you undoubtedly have seen newspaper men and "private eyes" make brilliant catches of clever and dangerous criminals while the police stand by helplessly or else are off somewhere chasing straws. This may be good fiction, but it is not the way crimes are solved. In real life the criminal is caught by a trained detective who through years of experience and observation has learned to diagnose a crook's modus operandi as accurately as a doctor can detect appendicitis.

The detective's job is seldom spectacular. Usually it is routine, monotonous and tiresome, but it gets results. Contrary to public opinion, disguises and subterfuge do not play an important part in detection of criminals. A detective's best weapons are his sources of information, the people he knows. And if he builds a reputation as a reliable police officer through the years he gets unlimited support from the public.

In every police department the top 10 per cent of the officers are the ones who catch the malefactors, find stolen cars, pick up runaway kids and somehow manage to be where they're needed. They seem to have an inborn capacity for police work. It is something you cannot learn in a classroom or out of a book. We send a man to school, teach him everything he needs to know, but he is not a fully qualified police officer until he has had at least four years of experience with people and their behavior.

People are a policeman's chief business. He has to judge them in many different moods, in grief, anger, panic and other emotional frames of mind. He has to handle them in situations which vary from simple to complex, from ridiculous to tragic, and know what he is doing at all times. He has to be sure of his legal position in case of an arrest, since every arrest he makes is at his own peril. He can be personally sued for false arrest if he does not strictly adhere to the law. He has to mingle with people from all walks of life, know their habits and understand human nature. Experience is his best instructor. The longer he is in service and the more diversified his experience the more value he is to the community.

Professional criminals are always on the alert for the retirement or promotion of detectives who have handled them. They know that once certain officers are no longer on their trail they can take up their illegal activity again and be temporarily safe from recognition.

Occasionally police have to deal with professional informants. This is not a desirable practice, but it is inevitable that certain people in the underworld in a metropolitan area will always have information on criminal activities and will sell it for a price. If it is a robbery or burglary in which the loss is substantial and a reward has been offered by an insurance company they will inform. Frequently individuals holding grudges against acquaintances, or jealous of them, will "squeal" to the police. Rejected suitors will inform on their rivals or on the girls who jilted them. I remember one fellow who evened the score with his girl friend's hostile mother by reporting her to the police for filing a false theft claim to collect insurance. When a husband loses too much money

211

on the horses or at a gambling table, nine times out of ten it is his wife who tips off the police as to where they can find the bookie or the dice game.

The public generally considers murder the worst of all crimes, but police officers do not necessarily agree. Many murders and assaults are committed in fear and panic and were not planned. I remember one quiet, normal husband whose wife ran away and got a job working as a domestic in Beverly Hills. He located her here after a two-year search and waited for her outside the servants' quarters one afternoon to plead for a reconciliation. When she appeared in company with another man and scorned her husband's appeal he flew into a sudden rage and cut her throat with a knife which he habitually carried as a butcher's assistant.

Many ordinarily law-abiding citizens become involved in crimes of violence through momentary panic. I have known highly respected professional men and women who have been hit-and-run drivers even though they had ample opportunity to stay at the scene of an accident and report it. When asked later why they ran they cannot rationally explain their actions. Police knowledge of human behavior often solves such hit-and-run cases. We once had a traffic death on a side street in the early morning under circumstances which indicated that the guilty driver, who had fled the scene, was someone who used the street as a route to work. Officers patiently watched the street in the days that followed, checking on cars. They soon noticed a freshly painted car going by, on which the paint job looked amateurish. An officer took the number of the car, checked on the activity of the driver and found him to be the man responsible for the fatality. On another occasion an automobile repair man drove away from a traffic crash and stopped his car far from the scene to inspect the damage it had sustained. When he discovered that part of his bumper and tail light were missing he returned to the scene of the accident to look for these parts. He was arrested when an alert patrolman saw him picking up the pieces in the street and fitting them to his car.

Police officers consider premeditated crimes far more reprehensible than murder and other acts of passion and panic. Planned crimes of violence and crimes committed for personal gain are the work of hardened, vicious criminals who should be temporarily removed from contacts with normal human beings.

Many people think police officers are fundamentally opposed to probation and parole. This is not true. The average policeman wants to see criminals rehabilitated, but he advocates that adequate supervision be given probationers and parolees until such time as they reestablish themselves in society. I know many convicted felons and men on probation who are now good and useful citizens. We have a leading business man who was once a famous swindler, an evangelist who was a hold-up man, an actor who did time for manslaughter, and a successful real estate man who served a term in a State prison during his youth. Frequently rehabilitated criminals will appear at headquarters to tell us proudly of their achievements as honest members of society, and we are happy to see them.

The type of parole and probation which police officers do object to is that given to professional and dangerous criminals who have demonstrated by repeated violations that they are not capable of living honorably. I particularly disapprove of leniency toward criminals who repeatedly commit crimes for personal gain—burglars, thieves, hold-up men, forgers and bunko artists for whom crime is a way of life. I would never recommend parole for a bogus stock promoter with a long record who moves from state to state seeking new victims. Such criminals deserve their full sentences. Sex offenders and narcotics addicts, of course, are always poor risks for parole or probation. The chances of reforming them are slim.

Students of criminal psychology agree that certain individuals have dual personalities and cannot be relied upon or reformed, no matter what methods are tried. Such individuals cause a lifetime of woe to their grieving families and friends for no other reason than that they have a criminal personality, an inborn biased outlook on life. They are self-centered, irresponsible and often vicious. I know two brothers, brought up under the same parental control and given the same schooling and advantages. One turned out to be a successful business man, the other is a repeated criminal offender.

A police officer has to be a guardian, a diplomat and, at times, a psychologist. People in trouble have to talk to somebody and an officer who is a good listener can sometimes help them. We have no psychiatrist's couch at headquarters but we try to render as much assistance as possible. During the years I have listened to hundreds of stories from people perplexed by personal problems. A movie star, for example, whose wife has left home is reluctant to report it to the public and is more likely to bring his trouble to me on a confidential basis.

In many cases, crimes can be solved by listening to people talk. Often I have had conscience-stricken visitors come into my office to describe an incident in which they said a "friend" was involved and ask me what I would do about it. Usually I find that my visitors are describing their own predicament and are only trying to soften the blow of being discovered. These people always tell me they feel better after making a confession. One day a stranger came in unannounced, sat down at my desk and asked: "What would you do to a guy who abandoned his wife and kids?" As I questioned him, I found out he was the man and was wanted as a fugitive. Another visitor came in to discuss methods of detecting check forgeries and how successful they are. His interest aroused my suspicion and we quietly launched an investigation which revealed he had forged a signature on a business document. I also have had visits from business men who suspect their partners of stealing from the firm and want to know what to do, and one of my callers recently wanted to know if I remembered arresting him 15 years ago as a gin-rummy card shark and that he had served time on a narcotics charge. All he wanted was for me to know that he was no longer an addict or a cheat. His girl friend was coming to town and he was taking this precaution in the hope that he would not be picked up by the police while she was here.

A married business man and his girl friend once brought an age-old problem to me. The man wanted to return to his wife, after a brief but warm romance with the girl, but the girl refused to give him up. She clung to him so tenaciously that he had threatened to commit suicide in order to escape from his trouble. My sympathies were with the girl, after hearing her tearful story, but I felt the only way to solve the situation was to talk to her like a Dutch uncle. "If this man commits suicide, you will be the one that's hurt," I advised her. "You wouldn't want that. If you think you have a legal case against him get a lawyer. But there's no law that can make him love you, and since he obviously doesn't, why not give him up?" After thinking it over for a while the girl agreed and let the man go. He left my office a chastened husband.

Police officers have to stand up and be counted on public issues and maintain certain fundamental ideals even if they are unpopular. After many years of dealing with the public a policeman knows an unsound idea when it comes along. When the Stockholm Peace Petition was circulated in Beverly Hills, we stopped it promptly, knowing that it was Communist backed. We know that too many citizens will sign petitions without reading them and let their names be used by groups whose real purpose is unknown to them. It is up to the police to prevent them from making such mistakes.

People have to be controlled, evaluated and guided by the police. Many otherwise law-abiding citizens have moral blind spots and have to be kept in line. Some years ago we were shocked by a report that some out-of-town high school students were getting drunk in a Beverly Hills hotel. When police arrived to investigate they found a graduation party, chaperoned by adults, at which alcoholic drinks were being served. The adults in charge were surprised at our negative attitude. "These high-school seniors can drink at home in our town. What's wrong with their drinking here?" they asked. Our officers replied: "We aren't responsible for what they do in your town, but while they are in Beverly Hills they are not going to drink!" The party quickly became non-alcoholic. This was not an isolated case of curious social behavior. It happened again when some local parents served champagne in their home at a graduation party for under-age students. These parents were educated and intelligent people, but they seemed incapable of realizing the moral danger of their action.

Through the years society has changed and with it the character of police work. The trend now is toward specialization, even as it is in law, medicine and other professions. I feel that this trend has developed a more mechanical attitude toward a police career than the oldtime officers had. In large cities, detective work is more specialized, with homicide, robbery, burglary, bunko squads and other units operating individually. In smaller cities, however, law enforcement officers have to be more general practitioners. In a city the size of Beverly Hills, a police officer gains a general knowledge of all types of crime, where the big-city policeman becomes an expert usually in only one field. The job of the Chief of Police is to see that there is coordination between divisions and to keep the trend toward specialization from getting out of hand. In some cities, traffic officers pay no attention to burglary unless it happens in front of them, and a man on the robbery detail wouldn't think of tackling a bunko case.

In many cities police experts who are unfamiliar with the department and the city have been brought in from the outside to be chiefs of police. Such appointees do not get the same cooperation from the rank and file as a man who rose from the ranks. This practice of importing executive talent dampens the enthusiasm of career officers in every police department where it happens. To get loyal and effective work from a department even the youngest rookie should feel that he, too, has a chance to be Chief of Police some day.

Curiously enough, while some American cities have adopted the European custom of bringing in outside experts to head their police departments, the trend in Europe may be toward the old American custom of training police chiefs up from the ranks. Scotland Yard, for example, which heretofore has been headed by distinguished military appointees who might not be experts in police work, is now headed by an up-from-the-ranks Superintendent, Herbert W. Hannam. In former days a rank-and-file officer at the Yard rarely got higher than Inspector.

Police problems have changed in Beverly Hills in 30 years. One difference is in the mobility of the population. People shift more frequently from place to place, and each move tends to uproot established customs and behavior of the families involved. New contacts and new environments sometimes cause trouble and increase the crime problem. With fast transportation available by land and air, criminals move swiftly from coast to coast and no city anywhere is insulated from crime. Years ago criminals tended to stay in certain neighborhoods and in order to nab malefactors who were on the move we had only to watch railroads, interurban lines and steamships.

Court procedures in Beverly Hills have improved immeasurably since the days when I was a patrolman. Before our Municipal Court was established, justices of peace, who were lawyers in private practice, acted as court officers and the police frequently had difficulties with them. It was a peculiar situation. They were judges in the morning and defense counsel in the afternoon. I often found myself in controversy with "judges" defending criminals. Even today the working of the courts is sometimes baffling. I have known of cases in which a defendant was found guilty in one court, yet in an identical case with the same evidence in another court the defendant goes free. Much depends on the background and training of the judge on the bench. One may be a stern moralist, the other more liberal.

There are many frustrations about police work, the chief of which is that despite the improvements we have made during the past 30 years in our methods the national crime rate is increasing. An FBI report recently disclosed that in a

217

10-year period the number of major crimes reported annually in the United States increased from 1,685,000 to 2,800,000, or three times as fast as the increase in population during the same period. And this occurred at a time when our national economy was at a high peak.

Such statistics are disheartening, but they are also a challenge to the men and women who devote their lives to law enforcement. Police officers, like teachers and the clergy, dedicate themselves to their careers. If necessary they are willing to make the supreme sacrifice to maintain law and order. In spite of danger, drudgery, low pay, slow advancement, legal harassments and what sometimes seems to be apathy on the part of the public, police work has a powerful appeal for them because they are protecting society, serving their community and upholding the law.